A TASTE OF FANTASY

A TASTE OF FANTASY

TWENTY TABLE SETTINGS
AND MENUS
INSPIRED BY TEN
OF THE WORLD'S MOST
DAZZLING PLACES

KEVYN DE REGT
WITH RAY ISLE

PHOTOGRAPHY BY
ANDRE BARANOWSKI

RECIPES BY JULIA LEE

FANTASY SETTINGS, LLC GREENWICH, CT

Produced by gonzalez defino new york, ny

Editorial Director Joseph Gonzalez

Art Director Perri DeFino

Designer Susan Welt

Copy Editor Anne O'Connor

Map Illustrator Oliver Williams

Food Illustrator Sondra Murphy

ISBN 0-9762473-0-5

Color Separations by Spectragraphic, Inc., Commack, NY

Printed in China by C & C Offset Printing

THIS BOOK IS DEDICATED to my sons, Eric, Ryan and Scott, and their father, Kenneth deRegt, whose support in so many ways helped make it all possible.

So many people contributed to the creation of *A Taste of Fantasy.* At the top of the list is my partner in this endeavor, Andre Baranowski, who captured my vision and rendered it so masterfully in his gorgeous photography. My heartfelt appreciation also goes to Ray Isle, who has an uncanny ability to channel my thoughts and translate them into effortless prose; Julia Lee, for her wonderful recipes; Sondra Murphy, for her delightful drawings; and to the editorial/design team at gonzalez defino for helping to turn my dream into the beautiful reality of this book. And last, but certainly not least, I'd like to thank the people and companies that helped us create our fantasy settings:

GREEK ISLES
Polyvios & Regina Vintiadis
White Knight Maritime S.A.
  Captain Constantinos Andreou
Selene Restaurant

VENICE
Ristorante Antico Pignolo
Vecchia Murano Glass Factory
  Stefano Piccinetti, general
  manager
Hotel Danieli
CAM vetri d'arte
Simon & Sarah, models
Dario Sgobbaro, for arranging
  everything

TUSCANY
Castello Banfi
  Elizabeth Koenig Pagliantini,
  hospitality director
Banfi Vintners
  Lars Leicht, VP public relations

ST. PAUL DE VENCE
Atelier Tholance
  Florence & Jean-Louis
  Tholance
Le Saint Paul Hotel
  Olivier Borloo & Charles-Eric
  Hoffman, owners
  Frédéric Buzet, chef
Café de la Place
Our friends Henri Priolo and
  Nadia and the entire village
  of St. Paul de Vence

BARCELONA
Icono Serveis Culturals
Monica Enrich, guide
Hotel Arts Barcelona
Alejo Amaedo (former chef
  of the King of Spain)
Galería Greca (antiques)
Carmen Viñas (laces)
Olga de Sandoval (antique red
  velvet chairs)

MOROCCO
Abdelhak & Ann Benis
Hotel La Mamounia, Marrakech
Restaurant El Yacout, Marrakech
Hotel Palais Jamais, Fez

NETHERLANDS
Antoinette J.M. Strengers, guide
Gusta Krusemeijer
Herenweg tulip fields

SALZBURG
Buberi Gut Restaurant
M. Kouarits, guide

ST. MORITZ
Badrutt's Palace Hotel
  Roland Fasel, general manager
Monique Steiner

INTRODUCTION

IMAGINE BREAKFAST IN A PROVENÇAL BOWER. Now imagine that seconds later—the turn of a page—you could be having lunch *al fresco* in a Tuscan vineyard. In these pages my goal is to take you places you've never been before, from sipping mint tea under a Berber tent in Morocco to dancing under the stars at a Venetian masked ball on the Grand Canal, then to give you the means to recreate those exotic worlds at home. These pages contain a breathtaking array of sumptuous table settings and menus, each inspired by the flavor and feel, culture and history of my favorite places in Europe and Morocco. At the end of each chapter are sections on the foods, wines and markets of the featured sites as well as a menu and recipes to complete the feast.

In a sense, this book represents my own fantasy, born out of idle thoughts I had while running Clementine, my home furnishings store in Greenwich, Connecticut. I'd long imported merchandise from every corner of the world, yet I had never even been to some of the places I found most evocative. As they say, thought leads to action: before long, I began contemplating a book… a series of chapters, each focusing on a specific locale, with introductory sections on the colors, sights, sounds, textures and flavors of the place. Two magnificent table settings would follow, each designed to instantly evoke the essence of the place. I combed my library of design magazines for inspiration, made phone calls to friends in far-off places, and gradually settled on the ten locales presented here. And as I envisioned the book, I drew on my sense of style and my experience in the creation and marketing of home accessories to conjure up table settings that I feel are not only feasts for the eyes but also treasure troves of design inspiration and entertainment ideas—so even if you can't hop on a plane to Marrakech or take a train down the snowy slopes of the Alps into St. Moritz, you can evoke the ambience of those places for your guests at home.

All of the table settings were created on-site by myself, my crew and our brilliant photographer, Andre Baranowski. I aimed for designs that were both simple and ingenious—a sunflower centerpiece for the Tuscan vineyard lunch, a coiled-rope placemat for shipboard desserts off Mykonos, a harlequin place-card holder for the Venetian *ballo in maschera*—and that would be easily adaptable to anyone's home. While the accessories we used in the photographs—the flatware, plates, textiles and centerpieces—often were sourced on location, I tried to choose objects that could be easily acquired, or at least duplicated, on these shores. Many are available at my Clementine's home furnishings shops in Connecticut and online at www.clementinesonline.com.

We began our journey in Casablanca on March 30th, and finished in England at the end of June, racing from place to place as we tried to capture the perfect moment in each locale. It was pure adventure: we worked and laughed and accumulated more memories than I'll ever know what to do with. I recall driving into the courtyard of our hotel in Tuscany in a rental car so loaded with boxes and dishes and textiles that no one in the car could move an inch—I'll always remember the poor porter's horrified expression as we began unpacking everything. And because we shot almost all of our settings in natural light, of course I can't forget Andre trying to get us to work faster, saying, "Ten minutes! Ten minutes! We're losing the light!" Somehow, in every city, he always managed to capture the perfect light.

Andre also said, "You know, we all understand the table. It's the symbol of friendship, and we all sit and eat at the table." I couldn't agree with him more. That sense of connection—to places and to other people—was part of the reason I felt compelled to create this book. I hope you will enjoy being my guest at the tables I've conjured up for you in *A Taste of Fantasy.*

We had so many wonderful adventures along the way. That's me (opposite, top), giving a final touch to a place setting in our tulip field outside Amsterdam. The middle photo is of Andre, ankle deep in the waters off Paros, shooting our lunch table. At bottom, the crew prepares for a nighttime shoot along the Grand Canal.

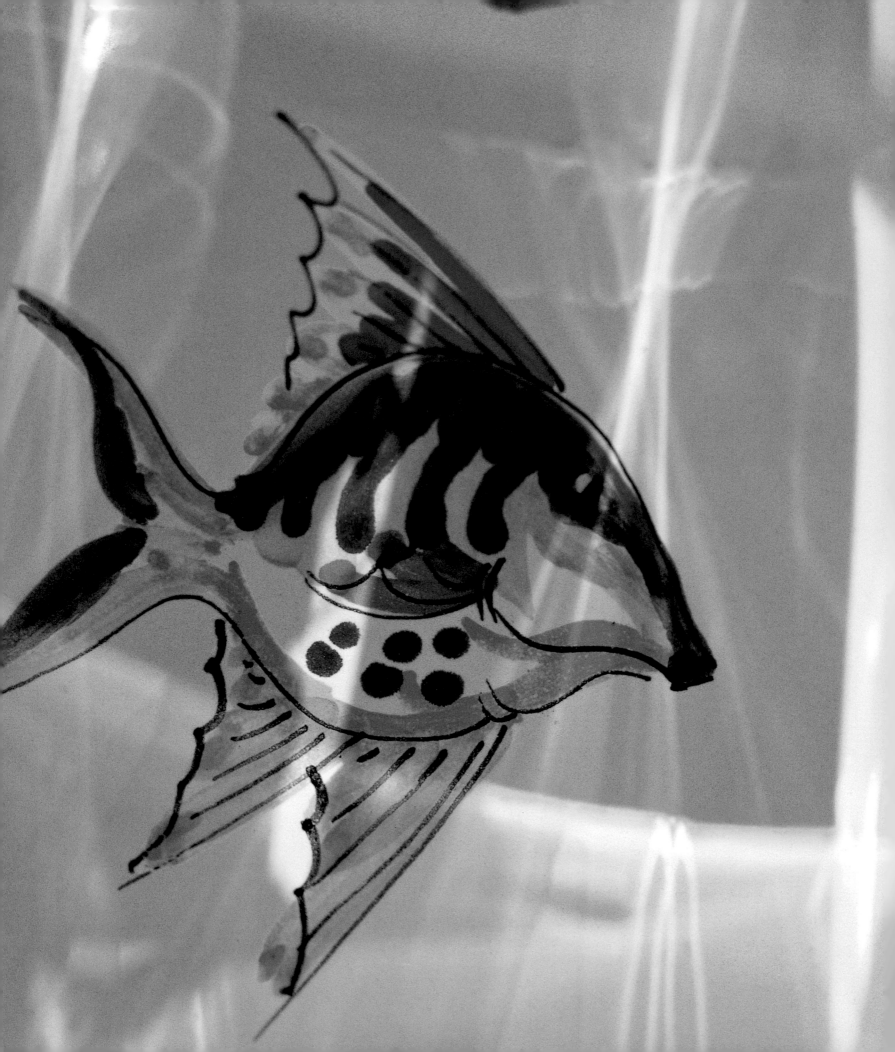

GREEK ISLES

*In Greece's sun-drenched
Cyclades Islands, time itself
seems to stand still*

CLIFFSIDE DINNER
IN SANTORINI

LUNCH ON THE
BEACH AT PAROS

SHIPBOARD
DESSERTS OFF
MYKONOS

Drifting among the Cyclades, the Greek isles of your dreams, you're free from everything but the sound of water lapping softly against your ship's hull or the feel of summer's heat sinking slowly into your skin as you lie on deck and await the next port of call. But there is history here, too. The Cyclades have been entrancing visitors for millenia, and their spell is still just as powerful today.

THE GREEK ISLAND LANDSCAPE

RANKS OF BLUE-DOMED ROOFS and dazzling white walls, perched on stony cliffs high above azure water—this could only be a town on one of the islands of Greece's Cyclades Archipelago. Scattered like a handful of glistening gems across the southern Aegean sea, the Cyclades are all rocky and steep. Some are occupied by nothing more than sea birds and the occasional stand of scrub brush, while others—Mykonos, Paros, Santorini and several more—are dotted with small villages and port towns.

The winters in the Cyclades are mild, but it's the summers that draw people here. In the summer months, the brilliant sun scythes away any haziness, outlining each building and rock with the kind of ferocious clarity that makes you blink. Up and down the narrow streets of the villages, cars, motorcycles, people and donkeys all negotiate for room to pass. Here a fisherman is selling local lobsters from the back of his boat; there a small shop offers artisanal cheeses and the local sausages, soaked in wine and hung from the ceiling to dry; and everywhere there's the casual rhythm of island life. No worries arrive here from other shores. Sitting in a café, looking out over the edge of the volcanic caldera on Santorini, you reach for a glass of the local wine and drink in the day. Soon the blue sky dims to orange, then nocturnal black. Have you lost any sense of what time it is? Well, does that matter?

CLIFFSIDE DINNER IN SANTORINI

THE TOWN OF FIRA, on Santorini, features one of the most dramatic views in the world, perched as it is high above the ancient volcanic crater, or caldera, that defines this place. We arrived on a June morning with the fierce sun blazing off the white walls of the town, so pure it almost hurt. And yet it also felt sustaining.

We arrived late morning to search for the perfect location for an early evening dinner. We found it on the terrace of a local inn, and with the permission of the innkeeper, we arranged a table and six chairs on a balcony overlooking the sea, facing west.

I wanted to create that sense of freshness mingled with timelessness that defines the islands. Nothing here is formal, everything is relaxed. Another way to put it: the bougainvillea blooms were harvested that afternoon—we hopped on a motorcycle and found them growing wild outside of town. But, of course, they'd also been growing there for thousands of years.

CREATING A SANTORINI TABLE

FOR THIS TABLE, I wanted to concentrate on the essential colors of these island towns, blue and white, so that even if you're at home, the setting will transport you to a place where gulls cry and the wind smells freshly of the sea.

We set up the table on a balcony overlooking the sea, after a hair-raising trip by donkey up the steep cliff to Fira. The blue pottery came from some of the local shops in Fira, and while the octopus pitcher and lobster plates didn't, they fit the mood I was trying to establish. The blue-and-white-striped silverware carries forward the table's theme, as do the clear blue-striped glasses, a perfect match for the pitcher. Even the chairs are striped with blue and white—all of which helps make the fuschia blooms of the bougainvillea such a vivid explosion of color. More bougainvillea blooms brighten each place setting.

The napkins (shown on the previous page) are a soft, waffled fabric, as white as the walls of our inn —in fact, the walls of all the buildings on Santorini. Finally, we used glass beads from a local store for napkin rings, a quirky, casual touch that seemed perfect.

LUNCH ON THE BEACH AT PAROS

CASUAL AND *SIMPLE* were two words that came to mind each time I arranged one of these tables during my stay in the Cyclades. And for the ultimate in casual simplicity, I thought, why not just place the table in the ocean itself? You could dine barefoot, feeling the breeze toss your hair and the water lap against your skin.

To continue this table's easygoing, watery theme, I placed a large glass bowl filled with water as a centerpiece, the base of it filled with blue glass rocks to add a sunlit sparkle to things. Floating blue flower candles were a nice addition, too. The tablecloth was soft white organdy sewn with pearls, twirled and flapping in the ocean breeze, and—intentionally—sometimes dragging in the water. We used actual strands of succulent seaweed for a decorative touch worthy of Neptune himself and a steering wheel from a boat we had found in the market in town, as a base for the centerpiece bowl. It was very catch-as-catch-can, but that was part of the point!

All of these seashells and sponges were purchased in the market in Parikia, the main town of Paros. The plates and glasses repeat the blue and white theme of the whole setting, and the silver fish dishes were just a fun touch, again a discovery from the local shops. I hadn't known I was going to use them, but the point was to use—and be inspired by—whatever was at hand.

SHIPBOARD DESSERTS OFF MYKONOS

IT'S HARD TO GET MORE NAUTICAL than actually being on a ship, gazing into the distance at the windmills that dot the shores of Mykonos, but with this setting I wanted to see what was possible.

Our captain helped out by providing a nautical chart to spread atop the brightly designed tablecloth, as well as ropes from the ship's stock that could be coiled to serve as placemats. An additional rope snaked about the table, encircling the blue glasses weighted with sand and shells that held the candles—ballast against the ship's constant movement. Finally, striped sailboat napkins carried through the shipboard theme.

I chose small pewter sandbuckets as serving dishes for ice cream, each holding about a quart, while a pewter boat carried a cargo of Greek pastries—*baklava, finikia, kourabiethes* and other delights. And at the end of the table, a bottle of ouzo, of course.

FOODS OF THE CYCLADES

THE CUISINE OF THE CYCLADES is defined by simplicity, just like life here: good, fresh ingredients in simple preparations that allow their vivid flavors to stand forth. And while this is not a wildly varied cuisine—agriculture on the islands is a difficult proposition—there is still enough depth to satisfy even the most jaded gourmand. The islands share many dishes in common with the mainland—*moussaka*, layered eggplant in a garlic-scented meat sauce, topped with a creamy custard; *avgolémono*, a simple but tasty egg and lemon soup (often used as a sauce, too); and *dolmades*, grape leaves stuffed with rice or meat. In general, island spices and seasonings are also similar to those of the mainland: thyme and oregano in particular, but also cumin, allspice, cinnamon and cloves, all testaments to Arabic influence on Greek cuisine. Lemon slices are a common accompaniment to almost everything.

In the islands as on the mainland, main courses are typically preceded by an array of small dishes (*mezethes*) such as kalamata olives and *fava*, yellow split peas pureed with onion, olive oil and lemon. Main courses tend to be grilled fish or shellfish, or vegetable dishes enhanced by a little meat. Greek desserts are modest, like *finikia*, honey-dipped cookies made with olive oil and orange juice, or *kourabiethes*, shortbread cakes filled with almonds and sprinkled with powdered sugar.

SANTORINI

If there's one food Santorini is known for, it's the small, intensely flavorful local tomatoes (chefs around the world know them for the quality of the tomato paste they produce). They're delicious eaten raw with salt, but even better in tomato keftedes, *or fritters. These can be as simple as tomato slices dipped in batter and deep-fried or they may be made of chopped tomatoes mixed with chopped onion and bits of wet bread, kneaded into a dough, formed into balls and then fried—either way, they're unforgettable. Also of note on Santorini are the* melitinia, *or cheese-and-honey pies.*

MYKONOS

Mykonos is such a tourist destination that you can get almost any cuisine you might want here—Chinese, Italian, you name it—but some of the local specialties still survive. Keep an eye out for louza loukaniko, *the local sausages, made from pork shoulder dried in the open air and seasoned with oregano, pepper and olives. It's often served in thin slices as part of a* mezethes *platter. Other local specialties include onion pies made with the island's* tyrovolia *cheese and* kopanisti, *a soft and strong-flavored cheese made of a blend of goat's and cow's milk.*

PAROS

The classic dish of Paros—similar to Greek staples like simple grilled squid or octopus stewed in red wine and then grilled—is gavros, *the local anchovies. These are traditionally sun-dried and then grilled, and they go perfectly with a small glass of ouzo.* Gouna *is mackerel that has been dried in the sun and then grilled (other fish to look for are* skaros *and* barbouni, *or red mullet). Paros also produces a soft, white goat's milk cheese called* mizithra, *which often takes the place of the more familiar feta in salads.*

MARKETS OF
THE CYCLADES

The Cyclades have been a tourist destination for years, if not centuries, and so many of the shopping opportunities are geared to the flocks of day-trippers arriving on cruise ships every morning. But the local population also has to eat and drink, and if you are willing to leave the most touristed streets (and towns), you can still find shops and small markets that offer more of a sense of the islands' true personalities.

SANTORINI

Fira, Santorini's main town, undoubtedly offers more jewelry stores than anywhere else in the Cyclades (except possibly Mykonos), but in the center of town, down the winding, narrow street, there is also a more traditional marketplace, where you can buy local produce like a basket of Santorini's justly famous tomatoes, or snack on the cheese-and-honey pie called *melitinia*. The town of Ia, on the northern tip of the island, is substantially less touristed than Fira though just as beautiful; shopping here is less of a game of dodge-the-tourist. And everywhere you'll see quaint local cafés, often with octopi hanging outside to dry in the sun, ready for grilling.

MYKONOS

Mykonos has become such a sophisticated tourist destination that you're as likely to bump into a Prada boutique—or one of the pelicans that wander the streets here—as you are a quaint local market. But if you sift past the tourist-trap junk—and bargain assiduously—you can find good deals on natural Kalymnos sponges, flokati rugs (made of wool from long-haired goats), hand-knit sweaters, *koboloi* (worry beads) made of wood or onyx, and the ubiquitous blue-and-white amulets used to ward off the evil eye.

PAROS

Parikia, the main town on Paros, offers a wide range of shopping choices along the agora, or open market street. Handicrafts, folk arts, food items and clothing are all available here; but there is also good hunting in the other towns on the island: Naoussa, Lefkes, Marpissa, Piso Livadi, Aliki, Prodromos, Ambelas and Drios. Of particular note on Paros is the pottery—it's generally agreed that the best ceramicists in the Cyclades can be found here. Paros is also known for its white, semi-transparent marble used in many of the architectural and sculptural masterpieces of ancient Greece, such as the temple of Apollo in Delos and the Venus de Milo in the Louvre.

ANDROS

KEA TINOS

SYROS DELOS MYKONOS

KYTHNOS

C Y C L A D E S

SERIFOS PAROS NAXOS

SIFNOS ANTI-
PAROS AMORGOS

IOS

SIKINOS

MILOS FOLEGANDROS

SANTORINI

WINES OF GREECE

GREECE HAS A WINE TRADITION that goes back thousands of years, and yet its wines are less well known in the United States than many far younger regions (like California's Napa Valley, to take an extreme case). And while there are plenty of uninteresting wines made in Greece and served in tavernas around the country, there is also an abundance of brisk whites and savory reds that can go head-to-head with anything the rest of Europe might offer.

SANTORINI

Santorini is a gorgeous place, but it also makes some of the best white wines of Greece. Grapes here grow on the slopes leading up to the old crater of the island's ancient volcano. The most widely planted variety is assyrtiko, which is typically blended with two other grapes, aidani aspro and athiri. It makes a vibrant, appealingly lemony, refreshing wine, often with notes of honey or nuts. It's eminently suited to the seafood-based cuisine of the Cylcades. Some of the best producers include Boutari, Argyros, Gai'a Estate, Sigalas and Heliopolous.

NEMEA

Nemea, in the Peloponnese, was until not too long ago a largely undistiguished region of cooperative-produced wines; now it's become one of the most exciting wine regions of Greece. The grape here is agiorgitiko (pronounced ah-gee-or-GEE-tee-koh), which seems almost perfectly suited to the valleys and slopes of this lovely region. Agiorgitiko produces wines that are juicy and rich, full of black plum flavors and plush textures. If you think Greek wines are all thin and sharp, this is the wine that will change your mind. Good producers include Gai'a Estate, Palivou Vineyards, Skouras and Mercouri Estate.

NAOUSSA

Located in the mountainous western reaches of Macedonia, Naoussa produces wines that are as rugged as the landscape, but they can also be as impressive. Primarily produced from the xinomavro grape (sometimes with a touch of merlot added these days), Naoussan wines are firmly structured, aromatic and tough—but served with something rich like braised lamb shanks they open up to a resounding richness. Moreover, they can age for years. The premier producer in the region is Boutari, particularly their Grande Reserve, but Tsantali, Ktima Voyatzi, Melitzanis and Nikos Fountis are also good.

If you don't at least try a glass of ouzo, then you haven't been to Greece. This aniseed-flavored liquor, with its deceptive potency and sweet taste, is a favorite everywhere in Greece. It's served at cafés, restaurants and bars, but particularly— and appropriately—at ouzerias. Many of the world's problems have been solved over several glasses of ouzo—what a shame that no one remembers the answers to those problems the next day!

RECIPES

SKORDALIA
(GARLIC AND POTATO DIP)

A classic Greek meze; and while it may not be the ideal food for a first date, it is delicious.

Serves 4

1	russet potato
2	cups cubed crustless country bread
4	cloves garlic, crushed and peeled
½	cup blanched almonds
3	tbsp. salt-packed capers, rinsed (optional)

Juice of 1 lemon

Freshly ground black pepper

½	cup olive oil

Salt

1 to 3 tbsp. half-and-half

1. Place the potato in a small pot, cover with water by 1 inch and cook over medium heat until fork-tender, 20 to 30 minutes. Peel the potato, pass through a food mill into a medium bowl and set aside.

2. Soak the bread in a bowl of water until very soft, then squeeze out excess water and transfer to a food processor. Add the garlic and process to a smooth paste. Add the almonds, capers, if using, lemon juice and black pepper to taste and process until almonds are coarsely ground. With the motor running, add the olive oil in a steady stream and puree until almonds are finely ground. Transfer the mixture to the bowl with the potato, season to taste with salt, (you may not need salt if you are using salted capers) and stir with a wooden spoon until well combined. Stir in the half-and-half to your desired consistency. Serve at room temperature.

TZATZIKI (CUCUMBER YOGURT DIP)

Made fresh, this will put to shame the tzatziki you're used to from the local Greek take-out shop.

Serves 4

1	cucumber, peeled and seeded
1	cup Greek yogurt
1 or 2 cloves garlic, peeled and minced	
1	tbsp. olive oil
2	tbsp. chopped fresh dill

Salt

1. Grate the cucumber on the large holes of a box grater. Using your hands, squeeze out as much of the cucumber juice as you can. Transfer cucumber to a medium bowl. Add the yogurt, garlic, oil and dill, season with salt and mix well. Cover and refrigerate until chilled.

SAGANAKI (FRIED CHEESE)

Serves 4

4	tbsp. olive oil
8	ounces kasseri or kefalotyri cheese, cut into 4 equal pieces

Flour

1	tbsp. ouzo
1	lemon, quartered

1. Heat the oil in a medium nonstick skillet over medium-high heat. Lightly dredge the cheese in the flour. Fry cheese, turning once, until golden brown, 1 to 2 minutes per side. Add the ouzo and ignite with a kitchen match. Swirl skillet until flames subside. Garnish with lemon wedges and serve immediately.

DOLMADES (STUFFED GRAPE LEAVES)

These are sometimes also made with a mixture of rice and lamb.

Makes about 30

½	cup uncooked Arborio rice
1	small yellow onion, peeled and finely chopped
3	scallions, trimmed and finely chopped
¼	cup chopped fresh mint
¼	cup chopped fresh parsley
¼	cup chopped fresh dill
¼	cup olive oil
3	tbsp. lemon juice

Salt and freshly ground black pepper

One 8-ounce jar brine-packed grape leaves, drained

1. Combine the rice, onions, scallions, mint, parsley, dill, 3 tbsp. oil and lemon juice in a medium bowl. Season to taste with salt and pepper. Set the rice filling aside for 1 hour.

2. Lay one grape leaf, vein side up and stem end facing you, on a work surface. Put 1 tbsp. of the filling just below the center of the leaf. Fold the sides of the leaf toward the center, then fold bottom up and over the filling and continue rolling until you reach the tip. To prevent leaves from splitting, do not overfill leaves or roll too tightly. Repeat process, making about 30 dolmades in all.

3. Line a medium-size heavy pot with 10 grape leaves. Arrange the dolmades in the prepared pot in a single layer, tightly packed together and in a concentric circle. Drizzle on remaining oil and ¼ cup water and cover dolmades with 10 more leaves. Place a glass or ceramic dish on top, cover pot and gently cook over medium-low heat until rice is tender, about 1 hour. Remove pot from the heat and set aside, covered, until dolmades come to room temperature.

GREEK COUNTRY SALAD

In the Cyclades, this salad also typically includes capers, or kapari.

Serves 4

4	tbsp. olive oil
2	tbsp. fresh lemon juice
1½	tsp. dried oregano leaves
1	clove garlic, peeled and minced

Salt and freshly ground black pepper

4	ripe tomatoes, stemmed, cored and quartered
1	green bell pepper, stemmed, cored and diced
1	medium red onion, peeled and thinly sliced
1	cucumber, peeled, seeded and diced
¼	cup kalamata olives

4 to 6 ounces feta cheese, cut into 4 large pieces

2	salt-packed anchovies, rinsed, filleted and patted dry

1. Whisk the oil, lemon juice, oregano and garlic together in a small bowl. Season to taste with salt and pepper and set dressing aside.

2. Arrange the tomatoes, peppers, onions and cucumbers on a platter. Scatter the olives and cheese over the vegetables and garnish with the anchovy fillets. Drizzle the dressing over the salad.

AVGOLÉMONO
(EGG AND LEMON SOUP)

Avgolémono is much loved throughout Greece; this version adds lobster for an elegant variation.

Serves 4

2	1½-pound live lobsters
4	cups homemade chicken stock
1	tbsp. cornstarch
2	eggs
⅓	cup fresh lemon juice
1	cup cooked long grain rice
Salt and freshly ground white pepper	
1	tbsp. chopped fresh parsley

1. Bring a large pot of water to a boil over high heat. Add the lobsters, cover and cook until they are just cooked through, 6 to 7 minutes. Plunge lobsters into a bowl of ice water to stop them from cooking any further. Remove meat from tail and claws. Cut lobster meat into small pieces and set aside.

2. Bring the stock to a simmer in a large saucepan over medium heat. Meanwhile, dissolve the cornstarch in ¼ cup water in a small bowl and set aside. Whisk the eggs together in a medium bowl until light and fluffy, then whisk in the cornstarch mixture and the lemon juice. Slowly add I cup of the hot stock to the egg mixture, whisking constantly, then return the mixture to the pot. Reduce the heat to low. Add the rice and season to taste with salt and pepper and cook, stirring constantly until thickened slightly, about 5 minutes. Do not let the soup boil or eggs will curdle. Add the lobster and cook until just heated through.

3. Divide the soup, lobster and rice between four warm soup bowls. Garnish with chopped parsley.

MOUSSAKA

If you happen to be in the Cyclades, try making this with white eggplants, a local delicacy.

Serves 4

2	medium globe eggplants, trimmed and cut into ¼-inch-thick slices
	Salt
16	tbsp. olive oil
1	medium yellow onion, peeled and chopped
1	pound ground lamb or beef
½	cup fresh breadcrumbs
½	cup freshly grated parmigiano-reggiano
1	large ripe tomato, peeled, cored, seeded and chopped
1¼	tsp. dried oregano leaves
⅛	tsp. ground cinnamon
	Freshly ground black pepper
5	tbsp. butter
3	tbsp. flour
1½	cups milk

1. Preheat oven to 350° F. Lightly sprinkle both sides of the eggplant with salt and set aside for 10 minutes. Heat 4 tbsp. oil in a large skillet over high heat. Add the onions and cook until browned, 4 to 5 minutes. Add the lamb or beef and cook until no longer raw, 3 to 4 minutes. Add the tomatoes, oregano and cinnamon, season to taste with salt and pepper and cook mixture until it begins to fry, 6 to 8 minutes. Set the meat mixture aside. Put the breadcrumbs and one third of the cheese into a small bowl and set aside.

2. Pat the eggplants dry with paper towels. Heat 4 tbsp. oil in a large clean skillet over medium-high heat. Fry the eggplants, in batches, until golden brown, 3 to 4 minutes per side, adding remaining oil to skillet as necessary. Set eggplants aside.

3. Melt the butter in a saucepan over medium heat. Pour 2 tbsp. of the melted butter into the bowl with the breadcrumbs and stir until mixed, set aside. Add the flour to the pan and cook for 2 minutes. Slowly whisk in the milk and simmer, stirring often, until thick, 3 to 4 minutes. Remove pan from the heat and stir in remaining cheese, season to taste with salt and pepper, and set béchamel aside.

4. Cover the bottom of a medium baking dish with one third of the eggplants. Spoon half of the meat mixture over the eggplants, spreading out to an even layer, and cover the meat with half of the béchamel. Repeat the process once more. Cover the béchamel with the remaining eggplants and sprinkle on the breadcrumb topping. Bake until golden brown on top, 45 to 50 minutes. Let stand 10 minutes before serving.

SEAFOOD STEW

To clean fresh calamari, hold the sac in one hand and firmly pull off the tentacles, then cut away and discard everything attached to the tentacles from the eyes down. Squeeze off the bony beak at the base of the tentacles. Now remove the quill-like, transparent bone in the sac and peel off the mottled skin. Wash the tentacles and the sac in cold water.

Serves 4

1½   pounds cleaned fresh or thawed frozen octopus legs

4   tbsp. olive oil

1   small yellow onion, peeled and thinly sliced

4   cloves garlic, peeled and thinly sliced

Leaves from 8 sprigs parsley, chopped

4   small calamari, cleaned

2   ripe tomatoes, peeled, cored, seeded and chopped

½   cup white wine

12   large heads-on shrimp

Salt and freshly ground black pepper

1   dozen small clams, scrubbed

1   dozen mussels, debearded and scrubbed

1   pound halibut fillet, cut into 4 pieces

4   sea scallops

1. Put the octopus into a medium pot and cover with water by 2 inches. Bring to a simmer over medium heat, reduce heat to low and simmer until fork-tender, about 3 hours. Transfer legs to a cutting board and cut into 3-inch pieces. Reserve 1 cup of the cooking liquid.

2. Heat the oil in a medium pot over medium heat. Add the onions, garlic and two thirds of the parsley and cook until onions are soft, 6 to 8 minutes. Meanwhile, separate the heads and tentacles from each calamari. Cut bodies into rings. Add bodies, legs, tomatoes, wine, reserved octopus cooking liquid and 1 cup water. Simmer, partially covered, until calamari is fork-tender, about 30 minutes. Meanwhile, peel shrimp shells, leaving the head and the end of the tail shells intact and set aside.

3. Season broth to taste with salt and pepper. Add the clams and mussels to the pot, cover and steam until clams begin to open, then tuck the shrimp and halibut into the stock. Simmer, partially covered, until shrimp are just cooked through, 4 to 5 minutes. Lay the scallops and octopus on top of the stew and cook until all of the seafood is fully cooked and heated, 3 to 4 minutes more. Gently stir to avoid breaking up the seafood. Divide the seafood and broth among four soup bowls and garnish with the remaining parsley.

YOGURT CAKE

This is one of the classic desserts of Greece.

Makes 1 cake

1½	cups goat's milk yogurt
16	tbsp. (2 sticks) plus 1 tsp. butter, softened
2½	cups plus 1 tbsp. flour
¾	cup shelled, hulled raw pistachios, lightly toasted
1½	tsp. baking powder
¼	tsp. salt
1	cup sugar
5	eggs, separated
2	tbsp. honey
¼	tsp. almond extract
	Finely grated zest from 3 lemons
3	tbsp. confectioners' sugar

1. Preheat oven to 350° F. Line a colander with a double layer of cheesecloth and set colander over a bowl. Pour the yogurt into the cheesecloth and set aside to let drain for 30 minutes. Meanwhile, grease a 10-inch-deep cake pan with 1 tsp. butter and dust with 1 tbsp. flour, tapping out excess. Process pistachios in a food processor until finely ground, then transfer to a medium bowl. Add the remaining flour, baking powder and salt and whisk until well mixed; set dry ingredients aside.

2. Beat sugar and remaining butter together in a large bowl with an electric mixer on high speed until light and fluffy. Add the drained yogurt and beat until smooth. Add the egg yolks one at a time, beating well after each addition. Add the honey, almond extract and lemon zest and beat until batter base is smooth. Beat the egg whites in a clean large bowl with clean beaters of an electric mixer on high speed until stiff peaks form. Fold one third of the dry ingredients into the batter base, followed by one third of the beaten egg whites. Repeat process two more times. Pour the batter into the prepared pan and bake until a toothpick inserted in the center of cake comes out clean, 55 to 60 minutes. Set cake aside to cool completely. Dust with confectioners' sugar.

YOGURT-AND-HONEY BIRD'S NEST

To look at the finished dish, you would think this recipe is complicated, but it's really very easy.

Serves 4

2½	cups Greek yogurt
4	tbsp. butter, melted
3	ounces katafi (shredded phyllo)
6	tbsp. honey, warm
½	cup shelled walnuts, toasted

1. Preheat oven to 325° F. Line a colander with a double layer of cheesecloth and place it over a bowl. Pour the yogurt into the colander; set aside to let drain for 1 hour.

2. Brush each of four 12-ounce bowls or four bowls in a muffin tin with a light coating of butter. Put ¾ ounce of the katafi into each bowl and gently press into the bowl to an even layer, allowing some to hang over the edges. Brush each with some of the remaining butter. Bake until golden brown on the edges, about 15 minutes. Carefully transfer the nests to a wire rack to cool completely. Put 1 tbsp. of the honey into the bottom of each nest, then spoon in some of the strained yogurt. Drizzle some of the remaining honey over each. Garnish each with a few pieces of walnut. Serve immediately.

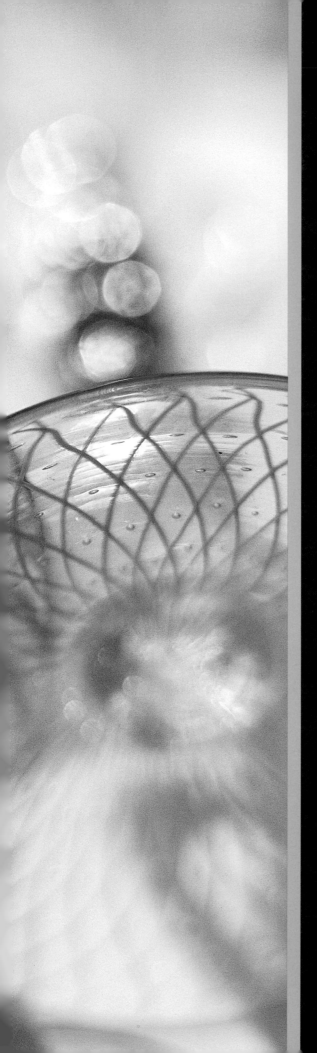

VENICE

*At night the mists
off the ancient canals shroud
a world of mystery*

BALLO IN
MASCHERA
ON THE
GRAND CANAL

Venice is the city of mystery, full of secrets and unanswered questions. Here, ancient canals weave their way along grand palazzos and crumbling monuments, and the people are famous for their love of masks and fascination with façades. Where better to spend an evening dining and dancing in disguise than along the mist-shrouded waterways of Venice?

THE VENETIAN CITYSCAPE

VENICE IS THE CLASSIC EXAMPLE of the whole being greater than the sum of the parts. Cross the Venetian lagoon from the industrial centers of Marghera and Mestre to the true city of Venice, and you'll land on one of one hundred and twenty islands, some great and some small, all defined by Venice's famous canals. It's a watery network plied daily by vaporettos and water taxis and the city's iconic gondolas.

Set foot on land, and you'll enter a maze of narrow alleyways, or *calli.* Eventually a canal will block the way, to be crossed by means of one of Venice's four hundred bridges. The most famous, of course, is the Rialto, which soars across the Grand Canal in the center of the city. That imposing waterway, the lifeline of Venice, is flanked on either side by marble and stone palazzi, faded by time into a kind of grand senescence.

In some ways, Venice is the most decrepit of Italy's great cities, and in other ways, it's the most vibrant—a curious mingling of romance and water-stained truth that leaves visitors ever so slightly disoriented. But is that surprising, in a city where land is water, and water, land? For many years Venice was slowly sinking into the murky depths—a process that has been stopped, for now. But who knows when it might begin again? Better to take your romance in the moment and not ask too many questions.

BALLO IN MASCHERA ON THE GRAND CANAL

I ARRIVED IN VENICE after the sun had set, and in the darkness of the Venetian night looked for the perfect location for our masquerade ball. I found it—where else?—on the Grand Canal.

I wanted the feel of a lavish masquerade ball in purple and gold, with that particular Venetian touch of mystery. The city obliged, as it has for centuries. Who are the guests? No one may ever know. They arrive by gondola, the gondolier in his striped shirt silent as the boat slips through the early evening air. The table is worthy of royalty, or of anyone pretending to royalty, but on this night who can tell the difference? The centerpiece orchids dip in the feathery breeze, the guests in their elaborate costumes dine and dance together, and then they vanish once more into the night. The masks never slip. No secrets are revealed. This is Venice.

CREATING A VENETIAN TABLE

WITH THIS TABLE I wanted to capture the subtle elusiveness of Venice, but also its almost gaudy extravagance. Everything is plush, rich, deep.

A different mask marks each place setting here, each purchased from a local mask-maker. The charger under each setting is a Venetian mirror—surely the artisan who made it never guessed it would be put to this use! A gold, oversized napkin with a shimmering, silky sheen is tied with a beautiful orange, gold and burgundy braided tassle that matches the tassles at each corner of the table; the colors keep true to the theme of the whole setting. I chose three Murano glasses for each place: water, wine and champagne. Each glass is unique, each, in a sense, with its own personality.

I draped the antique table with a gold satin tablecloth, topped with an antique purple velvet fabric, everything combining to create a mood that is formal and festive all at once. The entire setting has an extravagant vertical feel, causing the eye to rise up to the orchid centerpiece and the elevated masks, set on top of enormous candlesticks made of black wood, hand-painted with gold leaf.

The centerpiece is a harlequin-patterned vase, filled with purple and white orchids—easily the most seductive of flowers. The vase picks up on the cavalier attitude of the harlequin place-card holders, each gripping a handwritten place card. They almost seem to be watching the goings-on.

FOODS OF VENICE

Venice's cuisine is defined by the sea. It's a rare meal here that doesn't include some aquatic bounty, be it squid or cuttlefish; roasted branzino or *carpione*, the salmon trout found in nearby Lake Garda; stewed *bisati* (river-delta eels) or *moleche*, the delicious soft-shell crabs that appear on menus in spring and fall.

One might think that a handful of small islands surrounded by water might not offer very much in the way of fresh produce, but that's not so—the fields and rice paddies around the Venetian lagoon and the farms of the Veneto region offer the inhabitants of Venice a rich assortment of vegetables, fruits and other agricultural products. In the Asiago highlands, for instance, rows of beehives stand amidst fields of wildflowers, and that flavorful honey, of course, makes its way to the great markets of Venice.

Despite the influence of the sea on Venetian menus, meat is important as well. Venetians invented carpaccio, thinly sliced raw beef drizzled with olive oil, and are just as mad about their *fegato alla veneziana*, Venetian-style calf's liver with onions.

RICE

The local strain of rice, vialone nano, *is one of the great risotto rices (along with* arborio *and* carnaroli). *It's perfect for Venice-style risotto—a little more liquid than in other places, hence the term* all'onda *("on the wave"). The classic Venetian rice dish is* risi e bisi, *or rice and peas, but other local favorites include* risi e bruscàndoli *(rice and wild hop shoots) or* risi in cavroman *(mutton-flavored rice with cinnamon).*

PASTA AND POLENTA

Every kind of pasta is available in Venice's many small food shops, but the local specialities include bigoli, *a thick, robust, wholewheat pasta like somewhat thicker spaghetti, made in a special press called a* torchio *and often served with a sauce made with sardines or anchovies;* cassunziei, *a ravioli filled with ricotta, beets, winter squash or spinach; and* paparele, *a tagliatelle-like noodle. However, polenta is consumed far more often in the Veneto than pasta is. This cornmeal mush is a common accompaniment for all kinds of foods. The familiar yellow polenta is widely available in the city's markets, but look for white polenta, local to Venice and the neighboring Friuli region. Venetian cooks say that polenta just off the stove should have the texture of seta, or silk.*

CHEESE

The Veneto produces many kinds of cheese, all delicious. Some familiar (and not so familiar) names include asiago, *a sharp cow's milk cheese;* grana padano, *a white or straw-colored hard cheese with a characteristic grainy texture;* montasio, *a semi-hard cow's milk cheese with a yellow paste;* taleggio di soligo, *soft, buttery and full of flavor;* monte veronese, *a fragrant and slightly sharp cheese with a thin, elastic rind; and* provolone val padana, *a mild, semi-hard cow's milk cheese that comes in various shapes.*

FRUITS AND VEGETABLES

The areas around the Venetian lagoon produce an abundance of delicious fruits and vegetables. Many familiar items will taste like you've never had them before: keep an eye out for the delicious local white peaches, which inspired Harry Cipriani to create the

(continued on page 58)

(continued from page 56)

Bellini; and the region's justly famous white asparagus. Tender artichokes, an abundance of mushrooms dried and fresh, black truffles, superb ripe cherries and luscious strawberries are all available in season in Venice's overflowing markets.

RADICCHIO

Of particular note in the Venetian larder is radicchio—certainly the Venetians take particular note of it! Venice's three varieties of radicchio are used abundantly in soups, salads and risottos or served as a side dish, simply grilled or sautéed. The rosso di treviso variety is elongated and pointed, with a creamy, delicious flavor; castelfranco is deep purple and mellow; chioggia *looks somewhat like the radicchio we find here in the States, but is far less bitter.*

SEAFOOD

A list that could go on for pages. The Pescheria market is a great place to investigate the fruits of Venice's waters, though other markets are easier to navigate. Spider crabs, or granseole, *are a local delicacy, especially in* granseola alla veneziana, *a simple dish of boiled crabmeat pounded with a mortar and served in the hollowed-out shell with olive oil, lemon, pepper and parsley. In the spring and fall, when the male crabs are shedding their shells they're called* moleche, *and are possibly even more delicious. Snails are delectable cooked* with celery and served with polenta. Squid or cuttlefish (seppie) *are superb in pasta, stuffed or sliced into rings and fried, or stewed in their own ink. Squid ink (available in little packets) is the base for risotto nero. Other shellfish at the market include* cannolicchi *(razor clams),* peoci *(mussels),* garusoli *(spiky sea snails) and* schile *(tiny shrimp). Carp and frogs are brought in fresh from the nearby rice paddies, and cod is dried and salted and sold as* baccalà—*the basis of* baccalà alla vicentina, *a creamy, whipped dish of dried cod cooked in milk, with onions, anchovies and grana padano cheese. Finally, Venice has some of the world's best sardines. Try them in* saor, *a sweet-and-sour marinade of onions, raisins, pine nuts and vinegar.*

MARKETS OF VENICE

VENICE REMAINS a wonderland of intriguing shops—the cardinal rule of shopping here may be that if you see something you like, buy it, because you may never find that particular shop again.

For food, there are open-air fruit and vegetable markets every day except Sunday. You'll find vendors and their stalls on Campo Santa Maria Formosa, Campo Santa Margherita and Campiello dell' Anconetta. The barges moored by Campo San Barnaba at the top end of Via Garibaldi are also fine grazing grounds. Venice's premier market, however, is at the Rialto, which offers the kind of abundance that leaves one breathless. It's open Monday to Saturday from eight in the morning to one in the afternoon. Stop afterward for an espresso, or an *ombre*, as the Venetians call a midday glass of wine—you'll need it.

For handcrafted masks, visit La Venexiana Atelier on Campo dei Frari, San Polo, or Il Prato, on Frezzeria, San Marco. Wonderful handmade paper products can be found at Il Pavone, on Fondamenta Venier dei Leoni, Dorsoduro, or at Legatoria Piazzesi, on Campiello della Feltrina, San Marco.

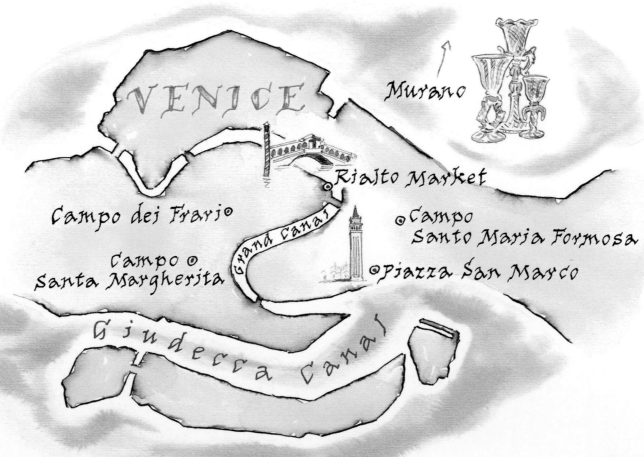

WINES OF
THE VENETO

THE VENETO REGION, for reasons that baffle those who have tasted its wines, remains an undersung sector of the Italian wine world. But some of the greatest names of Italian wine tend their vineyards in the hills near the Venetian lagoon.

PROSECCO

Nothing is more refreshing in the summer in the Veneto than a crisp, bubbly glass of Prosecco. This sparkling wine, most often drunk as an aperitif rather than as the accompaniment to a meal, is made from the grape of the same name. It's affordable and unpretentious, often with just the faintest edge of sweetness to its peachy flavor—a nice match for *prosciutto e melone* (prosciutto ham and melon) or the *tramezzini* (finger sandwiches) that Venetians are so fond of. Most Prosecco is quite affordable; consider bottles from Zardetto, Nino Franco, Bisol or Mionetto.

SOAVE AND RECIOTO DI SOAVE

Recent changes in vineyard technology, plus the ambitions of some of the top growers, have once again made Soave an Italian white wine to be reckoned with. Made primarily from the garganega grape, at its best it's a juicy, middle-weight wine with flavors of green melon and pear. Look for the producers Gini, Inama, Pieropan and Masi. And don't miss Recioto di Soave, the sweet dessert wine of the same region.

AMARONE

If there's one wine from the Veneto that deserves the encomium "great," that wine is Amarone della Valpolicella. Amarone is made from the same types of grapes as regular Valpolicella—corvina, rondinella and molinara—but the process is quite different. After harvest, the grapes are dried for a period of weeks, concentrating their sugar and flavor; finally they're fermented and made into wine. The result is rich and dense, with deep flavors of black cherry, coffee and leather. Amarone can age for years, but whenever you serve it, choose a nice dry cheese for accompaniment. Try Amarones from Masi, Allegrini, Speri, Tommasi or Zenato.

MURANO
GLASS

MURANO HAS BEEN THE CENTER of Venetian glassmaking since 1291, when the doges of Venice forced the industry to move north from the center city to a separate island, largely because of worries that the glassmakers' furnaces could set the city on fire.

Murano's glassmakers ruled the world (of glass) until the early 1800s, when the industry collapsed under the weight of taxes imposed by Venice's Austrian Hapsburg rulers. Not until 1866, when Venice became part of the Kingdom of Italy, did the industry revive.

Murano glass is renowned for its extraordinary craftsmanship and flamboyant design. Unfortunately, there are also a huge number of glass Mickey Mouses and other touristy junk items for sale on the island. But even the most unlikely shops often have one or two pieces worth considering. Two of the better shops are located around the Fondamenta dei Vetrai: Venini and Artigianato Originale di Murano.

Don't miss the Museo Vetrario, Murano's museum of glass, located in the Palazzo Giustinian near the island's center. It traces glassmaking from Egyptian times to the present day, with, of course, a worthy complement of superb pieces from Murano.

RECIPES

SARDE IN SAOR
(SARDINES IN SWEET-AND-SOUR SAUCE)

STUFFED WHOLE PRAWNS

RISI E BISI
(VENETIAN RICE AND PEAS)

FRIED SOFT-SHELL CRABS

CHOCOLATE TORTE

TIRAMISÙ

SARDE IN SAOR (SARDINES IN SWEET-AND-SOUR SAUCE)

A classic Venetian appetizer, perfect with a crisp glass of Soave.

Serves 4

4	tbsp. extra-virgin olive oil
3	white onions, peeled and thinly sliced
⅔	cup raisins
⅔	cup pine nuts
¼	cup white wine vinegar
Salt	
Vegetable oil for frying	
12	fresh sardines, cleaned and heads removed
½	cup flour

I. Heat the olive oil in a large heavy skillet over medium heat. Add the onions and cook until onions are very soft, 20 to 25 minutes. Add the raisins, pine nuts and vinegar, season to taste with salt and cook until the vinegar has evaporated, 15 to 20 minutes.

2. Meanwhile, pour the vegetable oil into a deep skillet to a depth of ¼ inch and heat over medium-high heat until hot but not smoking. Season sardines with salt and dredge in the flour, shaking off the excess. Fry sardines, in batches, turning once, until golden and cooked through, about 5 minutes per batch. Drain the sardines on paper towels.

3. Spread half of the onion mixture in the bottom of a medium casserole dish. Arrange the sardines over the onion mixture and spread the remaining onion mixture over the sardines. Cover and refrigerate for I to 3 days to let sardines marinate. Allow the mixture to come to room temperature before serving. Serve with grilled or fried polenta cakes.

STUFFED WHOLE PRAWNS

There's an easy way to tell prawns from shrimp—prawns have pincers like a lobster, while shrimp do not.

Serves 4

1	cup fresh breadcrumbs
2	cloves garlic, peeled and minced
4	tbsp. minced fresh parsley
3	tbsp. minced fresh basil
2	tbsp. extra-virgin olive oil
2	tbsp. melted butter
Salt and freshly ground black pepper	
12	large heads-on prawns
1	lemon, cut into wedges

I. Move the oven rack to the top third of the oven. Preheat the oven to 450° F. Put the breadcrumbs, garlic, parsley, basil, olive oil and butter together in a small bowl, season to taste with salt and pepper and toss until well combined. Set the filling aside.

2. To prepare the prawns, lay a prawn, legs down, on a cutting board. Starting at the point where the head shell ends and the tail shell begins, cut through the shell with a sharp paring knife or a serrated knife two thirds of the way through the flesh and down to the base of the tail. Repeat the process with the remaining prawns. Arrange the prawns, cut side up, on a baking sheet.

3. Fill each cavity with some of the filling. Bake until prawns are cooked through and filling is browned, 18 to 20 minutes. Serve with lemon wedges.

RISI E BISI
(VENETIAN RICE AND PEAS)

The rice should be softer and creamier than in risotto, but not to the point of being soupy.

Serves 4

6	cups chicken stock
3	tbsp. extra-virgin olive oil
2	tbsp. butter
1	ounce pancetta, finely diced
1	small white onion, peeled and chopped
1	cup arborio or carnaroli rice
1	cup blanched fresh or thawed frozen peas
9	tbsp. freshly grated parmigiano-reggiano
	Salt and freshly ground black pepper

I. Bring the stock to a boil in a saucepan over medium-high heat. Reduce heat to medium-low and keep hot. Meanwhile, heat the oil and butter together in a heavy medium-size pot over medium heat. Add the pancetta and cook until fat begins to render, about I minute. Add the onions and cook until soft, about 5 minutes. Add the rice and stir until each grain of rice is well coated in oil.

2. Add 2 ladles full of the hot stock to the pot and stir constantly until the rice has absorbed the liquid. Continue adding stock, 2 ladles full at a time and stirring constantly, until rice is al dente, about 20 minutes. Stir in the peas and cook until heated through, about 5 minutes. Remove the pot from the heat and add half of the parmigiano-reggiano and season to taste with salt and pepper. Serve the remaining parmigiano-reggiano on the side.

FRIED SOFT-SHELL CRABS

Soft-shell crabs in Italy can be as small as one to two inches in length, almost bite-sized, deliciously sweet.

Serves 4

1¼	cup sparkling water, cold
1	cup flour
	Salt and freshly ground black pepper
8	small or 4 large soft-shell crabs, rinsed
	Vegetable oil for frying
1	lemon, cut into wedges

I. Put I cup ice cubes and sparkling water into a medium bowl. Sprinkle ¼ cup of the flour into the bowl, stirring until a thin batter forms. Generously season the batter to taste with salt and pepper. Set the batter aside to rest for 5 minutes.

2. To prepare the crabs, lay the crabs, shell side up, on a cutting board. Flip the sides of the shells up toward each other and snip off the gills with kitchen shears. Snip off the eyes. Turn crabs over and remove the skirt flap.

3. Pour the oil into a large deep skillet to a depth of ½ inch and heat over medium-high heat until it is hot but not smoking. Dredge the crabs in the remaining flour, gently shaking off the excess. Dip crabs into the batter and fry, turning once, until golden crisp and crabs are cooked through, I½ to 2 minutes per side. Transfer the crabs to a wire rack set over paper towels to let drain. Lightly season to taste with salt while still warm. Serve with lemon wedges on the side.

CHOCOLATE TORTE

A tip: keep the almonds frozen, and it will be much easier to achieve a fine grind.

Serves 8

12	tbsp. plus 2 tsp. butter, at room temperature
1	tbsp. flour
8	ounces semisweet chocolate, chopped
¾	cup granulated sugar
6	eggs, separated
1	cup almonds, very finely ground
¼	cup brandy
1	pinch salt
¼	cup confectioners' sugar

1. Preheat oven to 350° F. Grease the bottom and sides of a 10-inch springform pan with 1 tsp. butter. Cut a piece of parchment out to a 10-inch round and place in the bottom of the buttered pan. Grease the top of the paper with 1 tsp. of the butter. Dust the buttered pan and paper with the flour, shaking out any excess.

2. Melt the chocolate in a medium heat-resistant bowl set over a medium pot of barely simmering water. Set the melted chocolate aside. Beat remaining butter and granulated sugar together in a medium bowl with an electric mixer until light and fluffy. Add the egg yolks, one at a time and beating well after each addition. Stir in the melted chocolate, almonds, brandy and salt and set the bowl aside.

3. Using an electric mixer fitted with a clean whisk attachment and set on high speed, beat egg whites in a clean medium-size bowl until medium-stiff peaks form, 2 to 3 minutes. Add beaten whites to the chocolate mixture, one third at a time, folding whites in until just incorporated.

4. Pour the batter into the prepared pan and bake until a toothpick inserted into the center of the cake comes out clean, 35 to 40 minutes. Remove the outer ring of the cake pan and set the cake aside on a rack to cool completely. Once cool, dust the top with the confectioners' sugar.

TIRAMISÙ

The origins of this dessert are more recent than you might think, dating back only to the early 1970s, at a restaurant in Treviso. Since then, however, it's become a timeless classic.

Serves 4

3	eggs, separated
1	tbsp. fresh lemon juice
15	tbsp. granulated sugar
½	cup sifted flour
¼	cup confectioners' sugar
6	ounces mascarpone cheese
2	tbsp. dark rum
4	tbsp. cocoa powder

1. Preheat oven to 375° F. Line a 9-by-12-inch jelly roll pan with parchment paper and set aside.

2. Beat 2 egg yolks, lemon juice and 12 tbsp. granulated sugar together in a large bowl until thick and pale yellow and set aside. In a clean bowl, beat 3 egg whites with an electric mixer on high speed until stiff peaks form. Fold the beaten egg whites, in thirds, into egg yolk mixture. Sift the flour into the mixture and fold until just combined. Pour the batter into the prepared jelly roll pan, spreading out to an even layer. Dust top of cake with confectioners' sugar and bake until cake is golden, about 20 minutes.

3. Whisk the mascarpone, 1 tbsp. rum and the remaining sugar and egg yolk together until smooth. Pour the mixture into a pastry bag fitted with a ½-inch star tip. Refrigerate until well chilled.

4. Peel the parchment paper off the cake. Using a 3-inch fluted round cookie cutter, cut out 8 rounds from the cake. Arrange 1 round in the center of four dessert plates. Pipe some of the mascarpone mixture over the cake and top each with another cake round. Pipe some of the remaining mascarpone mixture on top. Dust each with some of the cocoa powder and drizzle some of the remaining rum over each plate.

TUSCANY

Under the vineyard sun,
in the shadow
of an ancient olive tree

A TUSCAN
VINEYARD
FEAST

AN EARLY
EVENING
GARDEN PARTY

We arrived in Tuscany with the warm breeze coming down off the cypress-studded hills and the air scented with meadow flowers. Our destination the next morning was Castello Banfi, where we worked in the July sun to create our table settings: the first between the vineyard rows and the next under the shadow of an ancient olive tree.

THE TUSCAN LANDSCAPE

TUSCANY IS GREEN AND GOLD—the green of the hills, rolling softly into the distance as you follow a winding road, the gold of fields of sunflowers surrounding you on all sides. Here, the scented air streaming in the open window is as fresh as pine, as grassy and herbal as newly made olive oil rubbed between your palms, as rich as a truffle just uprooted from its dark hiding place in the earth. Listen, and you hear the cheerful clamor of a village market, the calls of wood-pigeons and nightingales, or, if you're lucky, the snuffle and then startled silence of a wild boar deep in a centuries-old forest. Tuscany is the feel of a knife pushing through the firm resistance of a well-aged piece of local pecorino, and the salty, creamy tang of the cheese as you taste it.

Landscape is more than pretty hills, though Tuscany has those in abundance. In a place with as much history as this, the people—what they've built, who they are—are as much a part of the landscape as the land itself. A stand of cypress trees may well have been planted two hundred years ago to define a property's boundaries; even a five-hundred-year-old olive tree grows where it does because someone once planted it there, intent on turning those dark, glossy fruits into precious oil.

A TUSCAN VINEYARD FEAST

OFTEN IT SEEMS that the only way to truly create the feeling of Tuscany is to dine outside. Maybe it's my memory of that sun-dazzled landscape, or the sound of the grape leaves whispering in the wind, but a Tuscan feast ought to be outdoors.

It was quick work to borrow some antique chairs and a beautiful antique table from our host's tasting room and transport them to the vineyard. There we were able to build our feast, surrounded by the rows of ripe sangiovese grapes awaiting harvest.

For our table setting we used local ceramics, many of them handmade at a little shop in Siena, like the water jug with its gold bands of Tuscan scenery. We chose a runner that repeated the gold colors of this place, and on it set fresh sunflower blooms we'd picked that morning from a nearby field. A pair of hundred-year-old wine barrels were our sideboards.

CREATING A TUSCAN TABLE

WITH THIS TABLE what I hoped to create was, in a sense, a distillation of everything that meant "Tuscany" to me. Of course it helped that we were in Tuscany in the first place!

First came the colors, red and gold, which set the theme. Local sunflowers placed in a line down the red table runner were echoed in the decorative work on the water jug and plates. The wickerwork chargers recall the straw covering on a classic *fiasco* of Chianti, Tuscany's most famous wine. We placed a large *fiasco*, on loan from our hosts, to the right of the table.

The tiles—made by local craftsmen, from designs taken off vinegar and olive oil bottles and salt and pepper shakers—mirror the landscape all around us. The centerpiece is a ceramic bowl from a little shop in Siena, filled with fruit bought from the local market in Montalcino that very morning: figs, plums, apricots, apples, nectarines.

And then, of course, there were grapes, right off the vines. They weren't ripe enough to eat, but they made a lovely addition to each plate.

The meal was simplicity itself. Fresh bread, salami and prosciutto, pecorino toscano and a piece of ripe raveggiolo. Figs, grapes, plums, pears. Bruschetta topped with chopped summer tomatoes and basil from the local market. Wines from the Banfi estate. For dessert, vin santo and cantucci, the region's crisp almond biscotti. Warm sun overhead. A gentle breeze. Nothing else needed.

AN EARLY EVENING GARDEN PARTY

FOR AN INTIMATE MEAL in the warm evening, we nestled a table near the trunk of a five-hundred-year-old olive tree, close by the castle walls. We hung a wrought-iron chandelier from a strong branch, and for a tablecloth chose a piece of velvet organza, as lush as the light filtering through the ancient branches. The centerpiece took mere minutes: a handmade green vase from a local ceramicist, grapes from the nearby vineyards, a few pheasant feathers—the mood of a place in a single gesture.

The meal was more elaborate than our vineyard lunch earlier that day: chicken liver crostini; pappardelle with porcini mushrooms; *bistecca alla fiorentina*, the classic grilled T-bone steak of Florence, drizzled with Tuscan olive oil; and for a light dessert, delicate almond meringue cookies.

The plates here recall the famous ceramics of Deruta, though in truth they're from several different towns. On top, the napkin's crest hints at the crests at the Palio in Siena, the legendary yearly horse race between that city's districts. And the chandelier may look extravagant, but it's truly very simple— brought straight from the market to the table that day, and inexpensive, too.

FOODS OF TUSCANY

THE HEART OF ITALIAN COOKING lies in the use of the freshest possible ingredients, and to that end, Tuscany offers a wealth of local produce. There are earthy (and earthly) delights, such as fresh porcini mushrooms and white truffles; staples like the chestnut flour that's used in so much of Tuscan baking; fresh fruit and vegetables—long, slender Italian radicchio; *cavalo nero*, Tuscany's famous black cabbage; and, in the summer, some of the best tomatoes on the planet. Tuscany's renowned bean repertoire includes white *cannellini* and the less well known (but perhaps even more

delicious) *piatellini*, either kind superb as the basis for a bowl of *zuppa di fagioli*—not for nothing are the people of Tuscany called by other Italians *mangia fagioli*, or bean eaters. Then there are the cheeses, such as *pecorino toscano*, *raveggiolo*, and fresh, milky *ricotta*, the latter an ideal dessert drizzled with local chestnut honey. Meat markets offer *salumi*, or cured meats, of various kinds, and at festivals in the summer there's *porchetta*, a whole roasted pig stuffed with herbs, delicious when it's carved off the spit and served simply on bread. Crusty on the outside and soft on the inside, Tuscan bread is traditionally made without salt. And, of course, there's always the luminous Tuscan olive oil—it's used on almost everything, and for very good reason.

MUSHROOMS

One of the finest edible mushrooms in the world, porcinis (or cèpes in France) are in season in Tuscany from August to November. With their glossy brown caps and fat stems—the name means "little pig," which they somewhat resemble—porcinis are wonderful sliced and sautéed in olive oil, toothsome and aromatic; when dried (this is how you'll usually find them in the United States), they add flavor to all manner of recipes. Less well known, but no less delicious, is the ovolo, or egg mushroom, so named because it looks like exactly that. Delicately flavored, it's best eaten raw, perhaps thinly sliced in a salad.

TRUFFLES

Dug up from their underground hiding places, truffles are one of the most sought after (and costly) foodstuffs in the world. While black truffles may find their finest expression in France, it is the white truffle that is unearthed in Tuscany. In the fall, accompanied by their pigs and dogs, the truffle hunters take their secret paths into the woods, returning, if they're lucky, with these light brown, frighteningly expensive fungi. They're best served raw, grated in thin slices over fresh pasta. And if you're in Tuscany in November, make certain you head to San Miniato for the annual festival celebrating the tartufo bianco.

CHESTNUTS

The areas around Arezzo and Lucca are celebrated for their chestnut production. A staple of peasant cuisine in medieval times, this starchy nut is so versatile that it has been referred to as the grain that grows on trees. These days chestnut flour is still widely used in Tuscan baking, particularly for castagnaccio, a chestnut cake flavored with rosemary and pine nuts, or necci, a flat cake made with chestnut flour. To make the flour, chestnuts are dried on straw mats for five to six weeks, then ground very fine. You can also still buy a cone of roasted chestnuts in most markets in the winter, to sample as you wander the stalls.

(continued on page 86)

Every small town in Tuscany has an
outdoor market, thronged on market days
with local people buying produce for
the week's meals. The air is aswirl with
the scents of fresh herbs, the eye dazzled
with brilliant red, ripe tomatoes, deep
purple cavalo nero, creamy white cheeses.
Wander among the stalls, then take a
break for a quick espresso or, on a hot
day, a cool cup of gelato.

(continued from page 84)

VEGETABLES

The range of fresh Tuscan produce is vast, something made clear to anyone visiting the region's food markets, like the Sant'Ambrogio in Florence. Everything from onions to spinach to broccoli rabe to herbs of all kinds is on display. Specialties include cavalo nero, *the Tuscan black cabbage that lends homey richness to the region's bread soup,* ribollita; *fresh sage, delicious fried as* frittura di salvia; *and wild fennel, whose roots, flowers and feathery leaves are used in different combinations in Tuscan cooking. And, in summer, Tuscan tomatoes are among the most delicious to be found anywhere.*

CHEESE

Tuscany, like any self-respecting Italian region, offers cheeses of various types—but undoubtedly the most famous is pecorino toscano. *Made from sheep's milk, or a combination of cow's and sheep's milk, it is sold young, fresh and soft, or aged and suitable for grating. Pecorino toscano is milder than other pecorinos, aromatic and lovely served with a glass of white wine— and ideal with ripe pears, a classic local combination.* Ricotta, *made from the whey left over after regular cheese production, is soft and moist when fresh, sweet with the taste of milk and perfect as a light dessert when drizzled with local honey.* Raveggiolo, *made from the whole curds lifted from the whey during pecorino production, bears a distant similarity to cottage cheese—but it's much more delicious.*

PORK

Tuscan markets offer a huge array of sausages, prosciutti, salumi, and other pork products. One classic is finocchiona, *a coarse-grained salami made with fennel seeds; another is* salame toscano, *a ground pork mixture studded with black peppercorns and large cubes of fat.* Prosciutto di cinghiale *is prosciutto made from local wild boars. There's also traditional soppressata—not the stuff you find on pizzas in the United States, but a flavorful, coarse sausage made from the head of the pig. And around Lucca, look for* lardo, *spiced pork fat that bears as much resemblance to lard as hamburger does to filet mignon—it's served sliced thin, often atop deep-fried dumplings called* gnocco.

BREAD AND PASTRIES

No Tuscan meal is complete without bread. Traditional Tuscan bread is made without salt, with a crisp outside crust and a moist interior; its mild flavor works well as a companion to Tuscany's full-flavored meat products. Tuscan bakeries offer a range of other wonderful breads, too. Schiacciata, *a flattened dough baked with olive oil, is what most American approximations of focaccia wish they could be; and look for* schiacciata con l'uva, *a grape-and-honey cake that's a harvest-time specialty in Chianti. On the pastry side, vendors in Siena sell* panforte, *a dense, sweet cake made with almonds, candied fruit and spices, and also* ricciarelli, *lozenge-shaped, soft almond cookies, irreverently nicknamed by the Sienese "nun's thighs." In Florence,*

look for schiacciata alla fiorentina, *an orange-and-egg-flavored cake dusted with powdered sugar.*

PASTA

Tuscans eat all shapes and kinds of pasta, but there are two forms that are local to the region: pappardelle, *a wide, ribbonlike noodle most often served with game-based sauces (usually hare or wild boar); and* pici, *a Sienese specialty, a kind of thick, short, homemade spaghetti.*

BEANS

The cuisine of Tuscany is studded with recipes for and including beans, among them the well-known cannellini, *a mid-sized white bean easy to find in the United States;* toscanelli, *small brown beans native to the region;* piatellini, *a smaller white bean many locals find superior to the cannellini, grown near Pisa and Lucca; and* zolfini, *pale yellow, thin-skinned beans with a creamy texture, much loved by connoisseurs. And, of course, springtime brings fresh fava beans to eat with a little salt and olive oil.*

BEEF

Tuscany is famous for its Chianina beef, a breed of cattle indigenous to the Val di Chiana. These massive white creatures are one of the world's oldest breeds of cattle. Bistecca alla fiorentina—*a grilled T-bone steak about two inches thick, seared on the outside and rare within, drizzled with good Tuscan olive oil—was traditionally made from Chianina beef, and still is in Tuscany's best restaurants.*

TUSCAN OLIVE OIL

TUSCAN OLIVE OIL is world-renowned, and for good reason. It's pungent and fruity, full-flavored and unmistakable in color—a kind of cold, beautiful green-gold. Its quality is maintained by rigorous control over the production process, and in November it's not unusual to see the pickers up on ladders, harvesting the just-ripe olives by hand with long rakes. A particular pleasure, though difficult to track down in the United States, is *olio novello*, sold within three months of pressing (that is, in November, December and January). It is brilliant green-gold in color, with a powerful grassy aroma and a peppery aftertaste. In the United States, for some good estate Tuscan oil, try those from Badia a Coltibuono, Tenuta di Capezzana, Castello della Paneretta, Castello di Cacchiano or any of the Laudemio oils.

MARKETS
OF TUSCANY

Every town in Tuscany, large or small, has its market. There's nothing more pleasant than wandering among the stalls—there are greens of all kinds, mushrooms dried and fresh, ripe fruit, sausages and cheeses, vegetables grown by the man or woman who's talking to you across the table. It's easy to find a picnic lunch or dinner in a flash, or to assemble the ingredients for a more sumptuous repast. And here, produce is harvested and sold when it's ripe, ready to eat; which means that while you may find perfect cherries one Thursday in June and not the next, when you do find them, they'll be like no other cherries you've ever had.

Besides food, local markets may offer furniture, paper products, ceramics or clothes. And, always, the nearest espresso bar is just around the corner, full of local people discussing the latest news—either of their neighbors or of the world. On a hot day, lounge a while at a gelateria for some of the best ice cream you'll ever have; or in the cool evening, stop for an aperitif in the town square and watch the world go by.

AREZZO

On the first Sunday of each month, visit the vast Antiquaria Fair; stalls are set up throughout the historic center of the city, selling everything from ceramics to antique clocks. There's also a food market every Saturday on the piazza Sant'Agostino.

FLORENCE

Florence has two main food markets, the Mercato Centrale, which is the largest, and the Sant'Ambrogio, both of which are open every weekday. On the second Sunday each month, the piazza Santo Spirito has fruit and vegetable stands selling seasonal produce. The Straw Market in late October is a vast Florentine sell-off of old (and sometimes valuable) furniture, furnishings and art.

LUCCA

On the third Saturday and Sunday of each month, the outdoor market in the piazza San Giusto offers a wide array of furniture, from rough-hewn country tables to elegant antiques. Each Wednesday brings the clothes market at the piazza Marconi, as well as a food market near the market of via Bacchettoni. And while you're there, don't miss having a cappuccino at the Antico Caffè Di Simo, one of Lucca's most charming coffee bars.

PISTOIA

Every Wednesday and Saturday, the busy market along via Cigliegiale features antiques, but also local cheeses and meats. There's also a busy food market on weekdays in the piazza della Sala, behind the cathedral.

PORTO SANTO STEFANO

Stop at an espresso bar to listen to wealthy yachtsmen and working fishermen debate who should have precedence in the marina here, then head to the harbor, where an interesting, though very occasional, market features furnishings from sailing boats and cruise ships. Not surprisingly, this seafaring town is also home to a great fish market.

PRATO

On the Saturday before Easter, September 8, and Christmas Day, visit the piazza del Comune for antique books and linens. The food market is open Mondays, on the viale Galilei in the Mercato Nuovo. Prato is also known for its biscotti, so don't forget to stop by Antonio Mattei's shop on the via Ricasoli for some of the best.

LOCAL FOOD MARKETS BY DAY OF THE WEEK

Most of the small towns in Tuscany have a main produce market open one or more days of the week. Here are some of them:

MONDAY

Bagnone; Castagneto Carducci, in the piazza del Popolo; Castelfranco di Sotto, in the piazza XX Settembre; Lido di Camaiore; Foiano della Chiana; Porto Ercole; Talamone; San Casciano in Val di Pesa, in the piazza della Repubblica; and San Giovanni d'Asso.

TUESDAY

Carmignano; Cecina, in the piazza del Mercato; Chiusi; Figline Valdarno, in the piazza M. Ficino; Massa, in the historic old town; Monteroni d'Arbia; San Miniato; Sansepolcro; Sinalunga, in the piazza Garibaldi; and Sorano.

WEDNESDAY

Bucine; Certaldo, in the piazza Boccaccio; Chiesina Uzzanese; Chianciano Terme, along the via della Pace; Pontremoli; Pisa, on the piazza Vittorio Emanuele II; Piombino; Pitigliano, on the piazza delle Fiere; Roccastrada; and Siena.

THURSDAY

Bibbona, on the piazza del Mercato; Camucia; Cascina Terme, on the piazza Mazzini; Empoli; Lucignano, on the via Matteotti; Pietrasanta; Poggio a Caiano, on the piazza IV Novembre; Tavernelle Val di Pisa; San Gimignano; and San Marcello Pistoiese.

FRIDAY

Castiglion Fiorentino; Colle Val d'Elsa; Follonica; Montaione, on the piazza della Repubblica; Montemurlo; Signa, along the viale Mazzini; Pienza; Portoferraio, on the piazza della Repubblica; Torre del Lago; and Villafranca di Lunigiana.

SATURDAY

Asciano; Castiglione della Pescaia; Castiglione d'Orcia; Castelfiorentino; Cortona; Fiesole, on the piazza Mino; Greve; Lastra a Signa, in the old town; Montopoli Val d'Arno; Pescaia, on the piazza del Mercato; Pontremoli; and San Vincenzo, along the via Vittorio Emanuele.

WINES OF TUSCANY

CHIANTI

Everyone knows Chianti, though not everyone knows that this familiar name is not just a wine—it's also the region the wine is from, between Florence and Siena, in Tuscany. Nor does everyone know that Chianti has risen in quality far beyond those years when it was defined by a big jug covered in straw. These days good Chiantis, whether from Chianti Classico (a subregion, not a designation of quality) or one of Chianti's six other regions, are rich and full of fruit, but still retain an earthy edge that recalls the land in which the grapes were grown.

BRUNELLO AND OTHERS

Brunello di Montalcino, made from the sangiovese grosso grape, is another great wine of Tuscany, aromatic, refined and able to age for years. For a sublime example, consider Castello Banfi's Poggio al Oro. For other Tuscan reds, look to Vino Nobile di Montepulciano and Carmignano, typically a blend of sangiovese with the French varieties cabernet sauvignon and merlot.

VIN SANTO

For dessert, Tuscany offers the wine of the saints: vin santo is a delicacy made from malvasia and trebbiano grapes dried over time to concentrate their sugars, then pressed. It's aromatic and rich, with a taste that recalls hazelnuts and dried citrus fruits—and it's ideal with a few almond biscotti.

Hundreds of Tuscan wines are imported into the United States, but a few producers to look for include, for Chianti, Badia a Coltibuono, Marchese Antinori, Felsina and Castellare. For Brunello—which is expensive—look to Biondi-Santi, Altesino and, of course, Castello Banfi. And for vin santo, try Capezzana.

RECIPES

TUSCAN CROSTINI

These crisply toasted slices of Tuscan bread topped with a flavorful chicken liver puree are a great beginning to any meal.

Serves 6

2   tbsp. Tuscan extra-virgin olive oil

1   small red onion, cut into ⅛-inch dice

1   salt-packed anchovy, rinsed, patted dry, filetted and coarsely chopped

1   tbsp. salt-packed capers, rinsed, drained and coarsely chopped

6   ounces chicken livers, coarsely chopped

¼   cup Chianti or other dry red wine

1   tbsp. balsamic vinegar

Pinch red pepper flakes

Salt and freshly ground black pepper

Leaves from 8 sprigs parsley, chopped

Six ½-inch-thick slices Italian country bread

I. Heat the oil in a medium skillet over medium heat. Add the onions, anchovies and capers and cook until onions are golden brown, about 5 minutes. Add the chicken livers and stir often until lightly browned all over and just cooked through, 3 to 5 minutes. Add the wine and balsamic vinegar and simmer until the sauce is thick, about 5 minutes. Add the red pepper flakes and season to taste with salt and pepper.

2. Transfer the mixture to a food processor and pulse to a coarse consistency, about 5 pulses. Add the parsley and pulse once or twice until just mixed.

3. Grill or toast bread on both sides. Cut toasts in half crosswise. Spoon some of the chicken liver mixture onto each toast half.

TOMATO AND BASIL BRUSCHETTA

For a simple starter, what could be better than chopped fresh summer tomatoes and basil from the garden, layered atop a lightly garlicky piece of grilled bread?

Serves 6

2   ripe tomatoes, cored, seeded and finely diced

Leaves from 1 sprig basil, thinly sliced

3   tbsp. Tuscan extra-virgin olive oil

Salt and freshly ground black pepper

Six ½-inch-thick slices Italian country bread

2   cloves garlic, peeled

I. Toss the tomatoes, basil and olive oil together in a small bowl. Season to taste with salt and pepper.

2. Grill or toast bread on both sides. While toast is still warm, rub some of the garlic onto one side of each toast, then cut toasts in half crosswise. Spoon about I tbsp. of the tomato mixture onto each toast half.

CANNELLINI BEANS WITH SWEET ITALIAN SAUSAGES

Tuscans love beans, using them in many local recipes, and white cannellini beans are probably the most famous.

Serves 6

1	cup dried cannellini beans, picked over
4	cloves garlic, peeled and crushed
6	sprigs sage
1	sprig rosemary
8	tbsp. Tuscan extra-virgin olive oil

Salt and freshly ground black pepper

6	sweet Italian sausages
1	small yellow onion, peeled and thinly sliced

One 28-ounce can whole peeled plum tomatoes, tomatoes coarsely chopped and juice reserved

1. Soak the beans in a large bowl of water for at least 4 hours or overnight. Drain beans and transfer to a medium pot. Add 2 cloves garlic, 3 sprigs sage, rosemary, 2 tbsp. oil and 6 cups water. Bring to a boil over medium heat, reduce heat to medium-low and gently simmer until beans are tender, 1 to 1½ hours, depending on the freshness of the beans. Generously season beans with salt and pepper; remove pot from heat and set aside for 1 hour. Reserve ½ cup of the bean cooking liquid. Remove and discard garlic, sage and rosemary, then drain beans and set aside.

2. Heat 2 tbsp. olive oil in a large deep skillet over medium-high heat. Add sausages and cook until browned all over, 8 to 10 minutes. Transfer sausages to a plate and set aside. Add the onions and remaining garlic to skillet and cook until onions are soft, about 5 minutes. Add tomatoes and canning juices and boil until liquid is thickened, about 5 minutes. Add sausages and reserved bean cooking liquid, reduce heat to medium and simmer until sausages are fully cooked, about 10 minutes. Pick leaves from remaining sprigs sage and add to skillet along with beans, season to taste with salt and pepper and simmer 10 minutes more. Drizzle on remaining olive oil just before serving.

PAPPARDELLE WITH PORCINI MUSHROOMS

Pappardelle are wide, flat noodles, ideal for a mushroom sauce like this, redolent with the concentrated flavor of dried porcinis.

Serves 6

1½	ounces dried porcini mushrooms
Salt	
1	pound dried pappardelle pasta
½	cup Tuscan extra-virgin olive oil
3	tbsp. butter
4	cloves garlic, peeled and chopped
Freshly ground black pepper	
Leaves from ¼ bunch parsley, chopped	
1	cup freshly grated parmigiano-reggiano

1. Pour 3 cups hot water over mushrooms in a medium bowl and set aside until mushrooms are fully hydrated, about 1 hour. Reserve 1 cup of the mushroom soaking liquid. Drain mushrooms, coarsely chop and set aside.

2. Bring a large pot of salted water to a boil. Stir in the pasta and boil until barely cooked through, 3 to 4 minutes. Meanwhile, heat the oil and butter together in a large skillet over medium heat. Add the garlic and cook for 30 seconds, then add the mushrooms and cook for 5 minutes. Reserve ¼ cup of the pasta cooking liquid. Drain pasta and add to the skillet. Add the reserved pasta water, ½ cup of the reserved mushroom liquid and season to taste with salt and pepper. Toss until the pasta absorbs the sauce and is fully cooked through, 3 to 4 minutes. Add more mushroom liquid if pasta absorbs liquid too quickly.

3. Remove skillet from heat. Add parsley and ¼ cup of the parmigiano-reggiano. Serve pasta immediately with the remaining parmigiano-reggiano on the side.

FLORENTINE-STYLE GRILLED T-BONE STEAK

Traditionally bistecca alla fiorentina *is made using beef from the great white cattle that graze in the Val di Chiana in eastern Tuscany; here in the United States, any good, thick T-bone steak will do.*

Serves 6

Three 1½-inch-thick T-bone steaks, left out at room temperature for 2 hours	
2	tsp. Tuscan extra-virgin olive oil
Salt and freshly ground black pepper	

1. Heat a grill to medium-hot coals. Rub the steaks with some of the oil then season each generously with salt and pepper.

2. Grill steaks, turning once, until well charred, 6 to 7 minutes for medium-rare. Transfer the steaks to a warm platter and set aside to let rest for 10 minutes before carving.

CANTUCCI
(TUSCAN ALMOND BISCOTTI)

These delicious almond cookies are traditionally served with a glass of vin santo, the sweet wine of Tuscany.

Makes about 4 dozen

5	whole eggs
2	egg yolks
¼	cup hazelnut liqueur
2	tsp. vanilla extract
2	tsp. almond extract
Zest from 1 small lemon	
4	cups flour
2	cups sugar
2	tsp. baking powder
2	cups raw almonds

1. Preheat oven to 350° F. Line two baking sheets with parchment paper. Whisk the whole eggs, egg yolks, hazelnut liqueur, vanilla and almond extracts and lemon zest together in a medium bowl and set aside. Put the flour, sugar and baking powder into the bowl of a standing mixer fitted with the paddle attachment. Stir dry ingredients on low speed until well mixed. Add the egg mixture, increase speed to medium and beat until a dough forms. Add almonds and beat until just incorporated.

2. Turn half of the dough out onto a well-floured surface. Flour your hands and shape dough into a 15-by-3-inch rectangle. Transfer dough rectangle to the prepared baking sheet. Repeat process with the remaining dough. Bake until lightly golden and cooked through, 30 to 35 minutes. Set the rectangles aside until cool enough to handle.

3. Reduce oven to 275° F. Using a serrated knife, cut rectangles crosswise into ¾-inch-thick slices. Transfer slices to the baking sheet, cut side down, and bake for 25 minutes. Turn cookies over and continue baking until lightly golden brown all over and very crisp, 25 minutes more. Cool cantucci completely before serving.

ALMOND MERINGUE COOKIES

These light Sienese cookies are called ossi del morto, *or "dead man's bones," because of their dry, crumbly texture. Despite the macabre name, they're delicious and easy to make.*

Makes 20 cookies

¾	cup sugar
⅓	cup flour
¾	tsp. baking powder
2	egg whites
1	cup raw almonds, coarsely chopped

1. Preheat oven to 325° F. Sift the sugar, flour and baking powder together in a medium bowl. Vigorously whisk in the egg whites. Stir in the almonds.

2. Line a baking sheet with parchment paper. Working in batches, spoon batter 1 tbsp. at a time and 2 inches apart onto prepared sheet. Bake until puffed and light golden brown, about 20 minutes. Repeat process with the remaining batter.

3. Let cookies cool completely on the parchment paper before removing.

ST. PAUL DE VENCE

Lavender scents the air and colors seem to glow under the Provençal sun

BREAKFAST IN A BOWER

DÉJEUNER SUR L'HERBE

FOUNTAIN-SIDE DINNER

*St. Paul de Vence has been
home to painters and poets,
socialites and movie stars,
but it's also — and always
has been — a simple place,
in the best sense. A good cup
of café crème, a basket of
fresh tomatoes, the fragrance
of orange trees and fresh
lavender, or the sight of
young and old playing boules
in the late afternoon light —
this is St. Paul at its best,
and at its heart.*

THE ST. PAUL DE VENCE LANDSCAPE

AS YOU LEAVE THE CÔTE D'AZUR and enter Provence—St. Paul de Vence actually belongs to both—you enter that magical border area between the Mediterranean coast and the sun-saturated villages of Provence. The freshness of the sea still seems to grip your skin, yet at the same time you feel all through your body the indolent, timeless warmth of Provence's vineyards and olive groves, its herb-scented fields and quiet forests of pine and oak.

St. Paul de Vence rises on a rocky outcrop a mere twelve miles from Nice, yet it might as well be in another world. The town began as a fortified medieval outpost and still retains a vestige of its early forbidding role—for one thing, unless you live here, you can't drive your car into town. But that's a blessing, really; St. Paul de Vence remains a walking place, where the pace of discovery is gradual and gracious.

Crush fresh lavender between your palms and inhale that heady, dusty, perfumed scent, or sip a glass of cool rosé on a summer afternoon in a village café. Walk a winding cobbled street between sixteenth-century stone façades to a fountain whose gurgle and splash will invest your dreams for the next twenty years. Moments like these abound here, as seductive and ripe as the fruits of the town's orchards and gardens. Pick one.

BREAKFAST
IN A BOWER

IMAGINE WAKING AS DAWN BREAKS in the soft air of the South of France, with the scent of citrus blossoms all around; now imagine someone serving you breakfast in bed—but the bed is in your garden.

The iron bed that sets the scene for this romantic breakfast came from a Paris gift show, actually. We set it up among the lemon, clementine, orange and kumquat trees that all grow on the property, and I draped it with lace to form a cozy canopy—this is a breakfast for two, after all. The flowers on the bed are lantanas (*lantana camara*, to be precise); we pulled the petals off one by one (a fun, but slow job) and arranged them in a checkerboard pattern. And the "bedspread" I fashioned from the vines that grew on all sides of the house—as the weather changes in the fall they shift to orange and finally flame-red. The breakfast itself was simple, as a good French breakfast in the countryside should be: brioche, croissants, fresh strawberries and oranges, good country butter, and, of course, hot café au lait.

DÉJEUNER SUR L'HERBE

TO CONTINUE OUR GARDEN THEME through another meal, we staged a light lunch in the middle of the vegetable garden. And in fact the garden served both as setting and as table setting.

The inspiration here was to use garden vegetables as bowls and plates, as decoration and as sustenance— giving a sense that the earth's bounty can be taken in unfamiliar as well as familiar directions. A head of cabbage was transformed into a serving dish for fruit fresh from the market: luscious blackberries, tart raspberries, ripe red currants (hard to find in the United States, but lovely in France), lush peaches. Canteloupe halves worked well as bowls for berries. We even used hollowed-out artichokes as coaster/cup holders. A cornucopia of fruits and vegetables served as the centerpiece, but, dramatic as that was, I had to admit it was hard to ignore the brimming basket of ripe tomatoes nestled by the side of the table; there's really nothing like a late-summer tomato fresh from the vine—so simple, and so delicious.

My youngest son once said to me, "Why does the worst nectarine in France taste better than the best one in the United States?" I didn't have an answer then, and I probably still don't—but I know he's right. The local markets of St. Paul de Vence and the surrounding towns sell fruit so fresh and ripe that to take one bite is to be transported.

FOUNTAIN-SIDE DINNER

I ADMIT, I HAVE A WEAKNESS for lavender. Maybe that's because it so inescapably brings me back to St. Paul de Vence and the fields of lavender in bloom that you come across, driving the little back roads around the region. Maybe it's because the scent is so fresh and so haunting all at once; and maybe it's simply that delicate, pastel color. But one thing I knew for sure was that our dinner by St. Paul's medieval fountain was going to feature lots of it.

I also knew exactly who I wanted to cook the meal: Frédéric Buzet, the brilliant chef of Le St-Paul restaurant and hotel. He created for us an astonishing menu: truffle salad, sea bass baked in Vallauris clay, sautéed fresh garden vegetables and for dessert, ice cream and fruit with a sauce I still can't describe except to say that it was transcendent.

CREATING A
ST. PAUL DE VENCE
TABLE

FOR THE TABLECLOTH in this setting, I used lavender silk, crisscrossed with layers of lavender ribbon; at its bottom hem we arranged a border of hydrangeas. The napkins were linen, with a handmade lace border. The lavender itself I picked that day from my own garden. I mounded up some of it for the cutlery to lie on, and used lavender French wired ribbon to tie fragrant bundles to hang around the table.

The dishes were very special, made in a family-owned shop just over by the fountain by my friends the Tholances. They're hand painted, and, to tell the truth, in all my travels I've never seen anything like them. (In fact the Tholances helped arrange this spot next to the fountain for us.) Three lavender glasses were set at each place, with lavender stripes.

While lavender unquestionably formed the theme of this setting, it's nice to have a touch of variety, in a shade ever so slightly different; that's why I chose the lavender hydrangeas and dahlias from my garden for this table's centerpiece, a silver-footed crystal bowl filled with all those flowers.

Lavender grows both cultivated and wild in the sunny, dry fields of Provence; its scent perfumes the air everywhere. We used bundles of sprigs and loose buds for this setting, but the flowers aren't the only lavender products to be found in St. Paul de Vence. Lavender honey is a rare treat, as is purple-colored lavender mustard; in fact there's probably no counting the myriad uses for lavender.

FOODS OF PROVENCE

THE CUISINE OF PROVENCE may not be refined, but it is honest. It offers infinite respect for simple ingredients, picked or harvested at the perfect point of ripeness, prepared in ways that allow the true flavor to shine. Provence means olive oil, garlic, tomatoes, eggplants; it means peculiar fish from the rocky coves and inlets like *rascasse, daurade* and *loup de mer*; it means the herbs growing wild and in gardens everywhere, perfuming the air with the lovely scent known locally as *garrigue*. Snails and truffles, so clearly of the damp and of the earth, are classic here; and lamb from the Camargue's salt marshes is justifiably famous—you can taste the herbs of the countryside in the meat.

HERBS

The air around St. Paul de Vence and the surrounding towns is as aromatic as if you'd crushed a handful of fresh herbs in your hand and inhaled the fragrance. Thyme, bay, rosemary, summer savory, cloves, tarragon, chervil, sage, marjoram and basil all grow in abundance here. And lavender, of course—look for the local lavender honey and mustards that are available in the markets.

TRUFFLES

Provence, especially the Vaucluse area, is one of France's black truffle hotspots (the other is Périgord; white truffles, however, are local to Tuscany and Piedmont in Italy). Rare, costly and richly aromatic, these underground-growing fungi are hard to find—specially trained dogs and pigs are used to sniff them out—and their season is limited, from Christmas until roughly March for black truffles. Truffles have an earthy, sensual and unmistakable scent and flavor, and this is the place to find the best.

VEGETABLES

Provence is a heaven for fresh vegetables. Eggplants, tomatoes, beets, garlic, mushrooms of various kinds, squash, zucchini and peppers are just a smattering of what you'll find in the local markets for use in dishes such as ratatouille, tian de légumes, artichauts à la barigoule *and others. And olives, of course, in abundance, from the tiny, flavorful niçoise to other varieties like salonenques, lucques and picholines.*

CHEESE

Provence specializes in both goat's and sheep's milk cheeses. Some of the best, which can be found in the local markets, are banon *(strongly flavored, wrapped in chestnut leaves, dipped in brandy or marc, and fermented for several weeks in a sealed jar),* camargue *(a sheep's milk cheese rolled in fresh herbs),* brousse *(fresh and creamy) and* roquefort *(the most famous blue cheese in the world, matured in caves above Montpellier).*

SEAFOOD

The Mediterranean provides a wealth of seafood for the South of France, and the locals make good use of it—you should, too! Look for daurade *(sea bream),* rouget *(red mullet),* loup de mer *(sea bass),* carpe *(carp) and* brochet *(pike), and then combine them in a classic bouillabaisse. There's no set recipe, but good bouillabaisse typically involves three types of fish, stewed gently in their own broth (and a good amount of wine) and served with some good* rouille, *a potent garlic mayonnaise.*

OTHER LOCAL SPECIALTIES

The markets of the regions around St. Paul de Vence are a wonderland of artisanal food items—sausages of all kinds, duck foie gras, fruit confits of clementines, prunes, cherries and apricots, black and green olive tapenades, biscotin *(the small, sweet cookies made in Aix-en-Provence), and the delicious* calissons d'Aix, *which are sweets made from ground almonds and candied fruits resting on a thin wafer.*

MARKETS OF PROVENCE

THE LOCAL MARKETS OF PROVENCE and the surrounding regions are innumerable and inexhaustible, always filled with people bargaining, buying and simply enjoying the myriad appeals to the senses. Most of the markets are weekly, occuring on a set day every week, though there are also annual fairs like the garlic fair in Piolenc or the linden blossom fair in Buis-les-Baronnies, and some of the larger, specialized markets, such as the fish market in Marseille, are open every day.

If you're in St. Paul de Vence, there's a small local market every day, but the nearest substantial market is in Vence, a short drive away. Every morning except Mondays, vendors set up inside the town's walls to sell fruits, vegetables, honey, spices and sundry other items. But there are also wonderful markets throughout the region. Here are a few of the best.

Cavaillon, on Mondays, is the place to buy the famous local melons at the source, but also fruits and vegetables of all kinds; this is one of the most fertile areas in a fertile land. On Tuesday, head to Aubagne, where they sell *santons*, the pottery crèche figurines the region is known for, but also other artisanal pottery and ceramics—the exceptionally fine local clay draws craftsmen from all around. On Wednesday, visit Buis-les-Baronnies. Even when the annual fair isn't on, this is still home to nine tenths of the linden blossom production in France, and a fine market for aromatic herbs of all varieties. On Thursday, head to Nyons—as the great Provençal author Jean Giono wrote, "Nyons to me is paradise on Earth." Perhaps he was referring to the town's famous olives and olive oil, as well as the luscious apricots. In the spring, the market in Carpentras, on Fridays, is redolent with the scent of the local strawberries and riotous with color from the flower stalls. On Saturday why not take in two markets? First, Grasse, the heart of the French perfume industry; this pretty market features lots of local, artisan-made food, but also a host of flower stalls around the central fountain. Then there's Arles, where two kilometers of vendors sell everything you could possibly imagine and more, including the garlic-laden sausages the town is known for. Finally, on Sunday, visit Toulon's market (which in fact is open every day), a heaven for vegetables and fruit fresh from the fields and gardens.

For a special treat, if you're in L'Isle-sur-la-Sorgue on the first Sunday in August, make sure to visit the floating market, when barges laden with goods pilot the river's pristine waters. One barge will have cheeses, another bread, another olives of all kinds; but it's the dreamlike atmosphere here that you will never forget.

Nyons

Buis-les-Baronnies

Piolenc

Carpentras

Avignon   L'Isle-sur-la-Sorgue

Nimes   Cavaillon

Arles

P R O V E N C E

St. Paul
de Vence

Vence

Grasse

Aix-en-Provence

Aubagne

Marseille

Toulon

Mediterranean
Sea

WINES OF PROVENCE

Provence and the Côte d'Azur may be more well known for their scenery than their wines, but in fact some very fine wine is produced here, from light, fresh summer whites to rich and powerful reds; the region is also the heart of France's rosé production.

WHITE

Though Provence does not produce white wine primarily, there are some appealing whites from Cassis—the appellation, not the black-currant liqueur. They're aromatic, fresh and appealing. Good producers include Clos Ste. Madeleine and La Ferme Blanche.

ROSÉ

Ah, rosé—no other type of wine seems so appropriate to the saturated sunlight of Provence and the seaside cafés of the Côte d'Azur. Rosés here range from light, simple quaffers from regions like the Côtes de Luberon or Coteaux d'Aix-en-Provence to more substantial wines from Bandol or Collioure. Good names include Château Routas, Les Clos des Paulilles, Château Canorgue, and, at the higher end, Domaines Ott, which produces arguably the finest rosés of France.

RED

A vast quantity of friendly, everyday red wine comes from regions such as Côtes de Luberon, Coteaux d'Aix-en-Provence, Côtes du Ventoux, and Coteaux des Baux, and some are quite good—names include Mas de Gourgonnier, Château Val-Joanis, Château Routas and Mas de la Dame. But the finest reds of the region are from Bandol—powerful, firmly tannic wines with a wild, earthy gaminess to their aromas, made primarily from the local variety called mourvèdre. A few of the best are Domaine Tempier, Château Pradeaux, Château Pibarnon and Château La Rouvière.

The wines shown at right, from Château de Jasson and Domaine de Revelette, are difficult, if not impossible, to find in the United States at the moment. But what a pity, for they are vivid expressions of the range of Provençal wines. Perhaps the answer is simply to take a trip to St. Paul, where you can sit at an outdoor café and try them.

RECIPES

PISSALADIÈRE
(PROVENCE-STYLE PIZZA)

PAN BAGNAT
(SALADE NIÇOISE SANDWICH)

RATATOUILLE

SALT CRUST–BAKED SEA BASS

DUCK LEG DAUBE

PORK WITH TRUFFLES

GRILLED APRICOTS WITH
LAVENDER CRÈME ANGLAISE

PISSALADIÈRE
(PROVENCE-STYLE PIZZA)

Somewhere between a pizza and an onion tart, this is delicious warm, but it's also good served at room temperature.

Serves 4

One 7-gram packet dry yeast

Pinch sugar

8   tbsp. extra-virgin olive oil

2   cups flour

Salt

4   large yellow onions, peeled and thinly sliced

4   cloves garlic, peeled and chopped

One 2-ounce tin anchovy flat fillets packed in oil

½   cup Niçoise olives, pitted

1. Dissolve the yeast and sugar in 1 cup warm water in a small bowl and set aside until foamy, about 10 minutes. Grease a large bowl with 1 tbsp. of the oil and set aside.

2. Put the flour, ½ tsp. salt and 2 tbsp. of oil into the bowl of a standing mixer fitted with the dough hook attachment. Stir ingredients on medium-low speed then slowly add the yeast mixture. Increase speed to medium-high and beat until a dough forms, about 5 minutes. Turn dough out onto a well-floured surface and knead by hand until smooth, about 10 minutes. Transfer dough to the prepared bowl, cover with plastic wrap and set aside in a warm, draft-free spot until doubled in bulk, 1 to 1½ hours.

3. Meanwhile, heat 4 tbsp. of the oil in a large skillet over medium heat. Add the onions and cook, stirring frequently, until onions are soft and beginning to brown, about 30 minutes. Reduce the heat to medium-low and cook, stirring often, until onions are deep golden brown, 20 to 30 minutes more. Season onions with salt, transfer to a bowl and set aside to cool.

4. Preheat oven to 425° F. Grease a heavy medium-size baking sheet with the remaining oil. Turn dough out onto a floured surface and roll out to a ¼-inch-thick rectangle approximately the same size as the baking sheet. Transfer the dough to the prepared baking sheet and gently press the dough into and up the sides of the pan.

5. Spread the onions evenly over the dough. Sprinkle the garlic evenly over the onions. Arrange the anchovies in a crisscross pattern over the top. Put one olive in the center of each anchovy diamond. Bake until golden brown and crisp, 25 to 30 minutes. Cool 10 minutes before cutting and serving.

PAN BAGNAT
(SALADE NIÇOISE SANDWICH)

A classic market-day snack.

Serves 4

2	tbsp. red wine vinegar
1	clove garlic, peeled and minced
1	small shallot, peeled and minced
2	tsp. chopped fresh parsley
6	tbsp. extra-virgin olive oil

Salt and freshly ground black pepper

Four 4-inch-round country bread loaves,
  halved crosswise

2	ripe tomatoes, stemmed, cored and sliced

One 8-ounce can olive oil–packed tuna, drained

4	radishes, trimmed and thinly sliced
1	green bell pepper, stemmed, cored and thinly sliced

Half cucumber, thinly sliced

1	small red onion, peeled and thinly sliced
2	hard-boiled eggs, peeled and sliced
½	cup Niçoise olives, pitted

I. Whisk vinegar, garlic, shallot and parsley together in a small bowl. Whisk in the oil and season to taste with salt and pepper. Arrange loaves on a work surface, cut sides up and with bottom halves closest to you. Spoon some of the vinaigrette onto the cut sides of each loaf half. Divide the tomatoes between loaf bottoms, then top each with some of the tuna, radishes, peppers, cucumbers, onions, eggs and olives. Cover each with top loaf and press down to compact layers.

2. Tightly wrap each sandwich with plastic wrap and set aside for at I to 4 hours. The longer the sandwich sits the better the flavor will be.

RATATOUILLE

There's no firm recipe for ratatouille, but this is a delicious one. Just make sure the ingredients are as fresh as possible, then serve with fish... or meat... or vegetables... or rice... or bread...

Serves 4

3	small eggplants, cut into rounds
2	zucchini, cut into rounds

Salt

10	tbsp. extra-virgin olive oil
2	yellow onions, peeled and sliced
1	green bell pepper, stemmed, cored and cubed
1	red bell pepper, stemmed, cored and cubed
6	cloves garlic, peeled and chopped
3	ripe tomatoes cored, peeled, seeded and chopped

Leaves from half bunch parsley, coarsely chopped

Leaves from half bunch basil, coarsely chopped

4	sprigs thyme
2	bay leaves

Freshly ground black pepper

I. Season the eggplant and zucchini with salt and set aside, separately, for 20 minutes, then pat dry with paper towels.

2. Heat 2 tbsp. of the oil in a skillet over high heat. Add the onions and cook until browned. Transfer onions to a heavy medium-size pot. Repeat the process with the bell peppers, eggplant and zucchini, cooking each separately in 2 tbsp. oil and transferring to the pot. Add remaining oil and garlic to the skillet. Add the tomatoes and cook until sauce has thickened, 6 to 8 minutes, and add to the pot. Stir in the parsley, basil, thyme and bay leaves, and season to taste with salt and pepper. Cover and cook over low heat until vegetables are soft but not mushy, about I hour.

SALT CRUST–BAKED SEA BASS

A variation on the clay-baked sea bass we were served in St. Paul de Vence, and a good bit easier to prepare. The salt crust keeps the fish nice and moist.

Serves 4

5   cups kosher salt

1   cup flour

2   egg whites, beaten

2   tsp. freshly ground black pepper

One 2½- to 3-pound whole sea bass, cleaned

3   sprigs parsley

3   sprigs thyme

2   bay leaves

Fronds from 1 bulb fennel

Half a lemon, sliced

1. Preheat oven to 400° F. Line a large baking sheet with heavy-duty foil and set aside. Mix the salt, flour, egg whites and pepper together in a large bowl until thoroughly combined. Add ½ cup water and knead with your hands until a crumbly dough forms. Pour half of the salt dough onto the prepared baking sheet, spreading the mound out to an even layer approximately the same shape as the fish.

2. Center the fish on the mound. Stuff cavity of fish with the parsley, thyme, bay leaves, fennel fronds and lemons. Pour the remaining salt dough over the fish, gently packing down to completely encase it. Bake 12 minutes per pound of fish. The crust will be a pale golden brown.

3. Set the fish aside to rest for 30 minutes. When ready to serve, carefully crack and remove the crust. Peel away and discard the skin. Fillet the fish and serve.

DUCK LEG DAUBE

Daubes are the classic meat stews of the Provençal region.

Serves 4

1   tbsp. extra-virgin olive oil

4   whole duck legs

Salt and freshly ground black pepper

1   ounce piece lean salt pork, blanched and cubed

1   medium yellow onion, peeled and minced

1   shallot, peeled and minced

1   large carrot, peeled, trimmed and chopped

1   rib celery, trimmed and chopped

2   cloves garlic, peeled and minced

1   tbsp. brandy

1½   cups dry white wine

¼   cup rich veal stock

1 bouquet garni, made of 2 sprigs parsley, 1 sprig thyme, 1 sprig rosemary, 1 bay leaf and 1 strip orange peel tied together with kitchen twine

1. Heat the oil in a large Dutch oven over medium-high heat. Season the duck legs with salt and pepper. Add duck and salt pork to pot and cook, turning once, until well browned all over, about 10 minutes. Transfer duck and pork to a plate and set aside. Pour off all but 2 tbsp. of the fat into a heatproof bowl, cool and discard.

2. Add the onions, shallots, carrots, celery and garlic to the pot with the fat and cook until vegetables begin to brown, about 5 minutes. Add the brandy and scrape up browned bits stuck to bottom of the pot. Add the wine, stock and bouquet garni, season to taste with salt and pepper and bring to a boil, then return duck and pork to pot. Reduce heat to low and simmer, partially covered, until duck is very tender, about 1½ hours. Remove the bouquet garni before serving.

PORK WITH TRUFFLES

Real truffles are expensive, but worth every penny.

Serves 4

2½	pounds pork rib roast

Salt and freshly ground black pepper

One 1-ounce fresh black truffle,
  cleaned and thinly sliced

4	cloves garlic, peeled and thinly sliced
2	tsp. olive oil
1½	cups rich chicken stock

1. Preheat oven to 325° F. Carve rib bones off the roast and set aside. Lay roast on a cutting board and make cut at the top along the length, 1 inch deep. Continue carving, keeping knife parallel to the board, unrolling the loin into a 1-inch-thick slab. Season pork with salt and pepper and cover surface with the truffle and garlic. Starting with a short end, roll the roast up, encasing the filling. Secure the roast with kitchen twine.

2. Heat the olive oil in a medium pot over high heat. Sear the roast until browned all over. Add the stock and reserved bones, cover and transfer the pot to the oven. Bake until internal temperature reaches 150° F on a meat thermometer. Transfer the roast to a plate and loosely cover with foil. Return the pot to the stove top and reduce the cooking liquid over medium-low heat until reduced by half. Pass the gravy through fine cheesecloth into a small pot.

3. This dish can be served either hot or cold. To serve hot, remove the kitchen twine. Carve the roast and serve with the hot gravy. To serve cold, pour the gravy into a small glass baking dish and refrigerate it and the roast separately overnight. Remove roast 30 minutes before serving. Remove the kitchen twine and carve. Cut the chilled gravy into cubes and serve alongside roast.

GRILLED APRICOTS WITH LAVENDER CRÈME ANGLAISE

Fresh and rich all at once.

Serves 4

1	tsp. culinary lavender
3	egg yolks
⅓	cup sugar
1¼	cup milk, hot
¾	tsp. almond extract
4	ripe but firm apricots, halved and pitted
1	tbsp. canola oil

1. Tie the lavender in a small piece of cheesecloth, gather the corners together, tie shut with kitchen twine and set sachet aside. Whisk the egg yolks in a heavy medium saucepan until thick. Add the sugar and whisk vigorously until thick and pale yellow. Whisk in the milk. Add the sachet and cook over medium-low heat, stirring constantly with a wooden spoon, until thick enough to coat the back of the spoon, about 10 minutes. Do not let custard come to a boil or else eggs will curdle. Stir in the almond extract. Pass custard through a fine sieve into a medium bowl. Retrieve the sachet and add it back to the custard. Cover the surface of the custard with plastic wrap to prevent a skin from forming and refrigerate until well chilled, 3 to 4 hours. Remove sachet from custard before serving.

2. Preheat a grill to medium-hot coals. Brush cut sides of the apricots with some of the oil and grill, cut side down, until lightly charred, 3 to 5 minutes. Serve apricots with some of the chilled crème anglaise. Garnish with fresh lavender flowers and blanched almonds.

BARCELONA

Gaudí meets Gothic
at the table
in Barcelona

SUNRISE BREAKFAST IN EL PARC GÜELL

DINNER IN A CLOISTER

Barcelona is both stern and playful, sybaritic and restrained—a magical mix of medieval grandeur and modernist whimsy. Nowhere is that mingling more visible than in the fluid, exotic work of Antoni Gaudí, whose architectural fantasies often seem to owe more to Alice in Wonderland than to any reality we know.

THE BARCELONA CITYSCAPE

BARCELONA IS A CITY OF RINGS. In the center lies the labyrinthine, crowded old town, the Ciutat Vella, bordered on one side by one of Europe's most famous boulevards, the Ramblas. Beyond the old town is the more orderly nineteenth-century grid of the fashionable Eixample district. Farther out still are the former villages, such as Gràcia, that once lay beyond the confines of the city proper. Scattered throughout are the distinctive architectural landmarks that define each layer of this elegant city's long history —from the stern Gothic grandeur of the Church of Santa Maria del Mar to the whimsical, undulating balconies and rooftop spires of Antoni Gaudí, Barcelona's most famous son.

And between those poles—the formal mystery of the church-influenced past and the stylized fecundity of Gaudí's wild imagination—lies the realm of Barcelona's style. Here, even the chocolates for sale in upscale boutiques are stylish—so graceful and pleasing to look at that you almost don't want to eat them. But, of course, you do. And as you walk the streets of the Catalan capital—noting the quirky Gaudí-designed tiles that line the Passeig de Gràcia, just as you note the solemn apse of the Cathedral, dating from the early 1300s—you take in both the city as it was and as it is, old-fashioned and avant-garde at the same time. It would be dizzying, in fact, if the people of Barcelona themselves didn't seem so comfortable with it all.

SUNRISE BREAKFAST IN EL PARC GÜELL

THE PARC GÜELL ON THE EDGE of the city is one of Gaudí's greatest achievements, where his riotous imagination takes full, surreal form. The views here reach down to the ocean, giving a sense of space against which Gaudí's twisting forms play; even the park's exterior walls are covered with bright mosaic tiles of Gaudí's making.

We arrived in Barcelona enlivened after a few days' rest in Provence, and a good thing, too. For this sunrise breakfast, I wanted the setting of the table to mirror the setting of the park, the colors wildly over the top: hot pink, bright yellow, radiant orange. But first, of course, we had to spend a whirlwind day securing the Gaudí-designed chairs in the city's antiques district, getting permits to shoot in the park, finding fresh flowers by the cartload, locating the clever little flower candles that ring the centerpiece. All great fun, of course—just as a breakfast like this should be.

CREATING A
BARCELONA TABLE

TO MAKE A GESTURE TOWARD Gaudí's modernist style, we used black, glass and chrome on everything on the table—except for the riotously colored flowers, of course. The table itself we parked right in front of a giant mosaic lizard—an emblem that's come to represent Gaudí and is reproduced throughout the city. And in a spirit of light surrealism I chose to incorporate as many kitchen utensils as possible into the overall design. A whisk, for instance, served as a napkin-tie; a skillet as a charger for the plates. Flour and sugar containers were our vases.

I chose a silk organza cloth in sage green as a tablecloth; the green beaded trim seemed to echo the sparkling chips of mosaic all around us. The brightly colored flowers purchased at the market that morning added life, certainly, but also brought a nice counterpoint to the more austere, modernist aspects of the table—the black lacquer tea trays under the chargers, the angularity of the arrangement itself, even the quirky pitcher with its doughnut-hole-like middle.

Finally the table was finished off with white cotton sateen napkins, a gerber daisy knotted in the kitchen-whisk napkin ring, a simple touch of gaiety.

DINNER IN A CLOISTER

IF THERE'S ONE TIP I have to offer in this book, it's never try to arrange a dinner in a cathedral. Recreate it at home by all means, but unless you like filling out a thousand different permits for one event, leave the real cathedrals to people who don't know any better, like us.

But though I was keen to create this meal in the Barcelona Cathedral's cloister, it's really the table setting that matters, not all that centuries-old stone. Two antique tables placed side-by-side made a palette for a deep green tablecloth with colorful embroidered flowers. Atop that, antique andirons create a candelabra decorated with pillar candles and red roses. Black silverware with silver detail, black lace napkins from a well-known lace shop in town, and square metal chargers with red rose borders all give an elegant sense of romance, as though this were the sort of dinner knights might have had before riding out on errantry. Even the hand-painted tile for serving tapas seems as though it might have come from that era.

FOODS OF CATALUNYA

THE MOST IMPORTANT THING to know about the cuisine of Catalunya is that, regardless of main ingredient, its overall character derives from four basic sauces. These aren't sauces in the French sense, though, but more the bases for actual sauces, or flavoring notes that provide a constant refrain throughout the cuisine.

The first, *allioli*, is a garlic-and-oil emulsion, mostly (and very frequently) used as a condiment. The second, *picada*, is a paste of ground garlic, almonds, bread and oil, used as a base for further sauces. The third, *sofregit*, is a sauce base made by cooking onions, tomatoes and often other herbs or vegetables down to an almost pasty consistency. Finally there's *samfaina*, a mix of vegetables sometimes used as a sauce and sometimes as a condiment. The observant diner will find all of these used throughout the Barcelona region.

RICE AND PASTA

While paella isn't technically Catalan (though you'll find plenty of paellas in Barcelona), arròs negre, *or black rice, is; and it's delicious. Colored by cuttlefish ink to a midnight blackness and studded with fresh fish and shellfish, it's a highlight of Catalan cuisine. If you're down by the water, another classic is* fideuà, *essentially a paella made with short noodles, toasted first and then cooked in fish stock.*

VEGETABLES

A good green salad is a rare sight in Barcelona, but some vegetable dishes here are delicious. Look for calcots amb romesco, *essentially a largish type of green onion, charcoal-roasted and served with romesco sauce;* escalivada, *or grilled red peppers and eggplants served with olive oil, salt and garlic;* espinacas a la Catalana, *spinach with raisins and pine nuts; and, though not quite a vegetable, the ubiquitous* pa amb tomaquet, *or bread rubbed with tomato and garlic, then drizzled with olive oil.*

SEAFOOD AND SHELLFISH

Barcelona is a seafood lover's paradise. Fishing ports line the coast to the north and south of the city, and the residents benefit from this bounty. You'll find fresh monkfish, daurade and hake from the Mediterranean; trout from the rivers of the Pyrenees; llagostas, *or spiny lobsters; the inescapable* bacallà, *or salted cod; and many other familiar creatures, like* coquinas, *or tiny clams;* chipirones, *or baby squid; and* espardenyes, *or sea cucumber.*

MUSHROOMS

Stop by certain stalls in Barcelona's Boqueria market, and you'll be overwhelmed by the rich, earthy scent of wild mushrooms, mounded in heaps and sold by the kilo. Many varieties are available: familiar ones like fresh porcinis, chanterelles and morels, along with exotic offerings such as yellow-gilled ou de reigs, *or compelling* rovel-lós, *which are the color of an old bronze pot—but far more tasty.*

GAME AND MEAT

The primary meat used in Catalan cuisine is pork, though lamb, beef and poultry are not absent. But the pig is king, whether turned into sausages—nearly twenty different varieties—ground and stuffed into squid or peppers, served as chops or loin roasts, or presented in any of what sometimes seems an uncountable range of preparations. Game is popular here, too—hare and venison, partridge, quail, wild pigeon, wild duck and woodcock—all of which can be found, fresh, in the stalls of La Boqueria.

MARKETS
OF BARCELONA

BARCELONA IS HOME to many markets—the huge flea market, Els Encants Vells, for instance, or the Sunday morning coin-and-stamp market in Plaça Reial; but there's only one food market that really matters: the Mercato de Sant Joseph, better known as La Boqueria.

La Boqueria is one of the great food markets of Europe, right up there with such storied places as the Rue Mouffetard in Paris, Les Halles de Lyon, La Pescheria in Venice and the Viktualienmarkt in Munich. La Boqueria is the largest of six main covered markets in Barcelona, and owes its proper name to the street it's on—but no one calls it Sant Joseph anymore.

The building that houses La Boqueria market is a remarkable wrought-iron structure, completed in 1870, with high columns supporting a vaulted rooftop of metal struts. On a sunny day, light streams in suggestively, giving the interior dimness a romantic cast. And the entire thing—this enormous, eye-defying space—is jammed with market stalls, and with shoppers. In some ways, the variety of people on display at

La Boqueria is as intriguing as the endless pyramids of produce (though, of course, you can't take the people home and cook them!). But as for foodstuffs, the variety is truly breathtaking. One stall may offer wild and dried mushrooms, seemingly fifty different kinds; another specializes in olives and olive oils, again in extravagant variety. Here are pyramids of candied fruit, in day-glo shades of orange, red and yellow; next door, vegetables and fresh fruits are just as vivid—glossy purple eggplants, deep red cherries, lettuce in a hundred different shades of green. Venture farther into the market and you'll find purveyors of meat and game, offering ducks and geese *(oca amb naps,* or goose with turnips, is a classic Catalan dish), blocks of homemade terrines and pâtés, and different grades of *jamón, serrano* and otherwise. Then there are the fishmongers, their catch brought in straight off the boat that morning—finfish of all kinds, prawns and shrimp, Mediterranean spiny lobsters still crawling around in distinct confusion at their new whereabouts. La Boqueria is inexhaustible, it seems, but it may well exhaust the casual shopper—so, for a breather, stop at the Bar Pinoxto for a quick coffee (or if you're feeling tough, a *carajillo,* essentially an espresso spiked with a shot of brandy that's a favorite of Catalan truckdrivers). And then? Back into the fray.

WINES OF CATALUNYA

CATALAN VINEYARDS provide some of the best wines of Spain, everything from vivacious and affordable sparkling wines to the formidable—and quite expensive—wines of the Priorat, much loved by wine collectors everywhere.

CAVA

The Penedès region grows the grapes for Cava, Spain's well-known sparkling wine. A refreshing alternative to Champagne (and much easier on the pocketbook), Cava is made in the same manner as Champagne, with the secondary fermentation occurring in the bottle—a technique that results in subtle, elegant wines. There are numerous producers. Freixenet is undoubtedly the most well known in America, but also look for Cavas from Cordoníu, Gramona, Juvé y Camps, Parxet, Jaume Serra and Segura Viudas.

TABLE WINES

The wine regions around Barcelona—Penedès, Alella, Ampurdan–Costa Brava, Conca de Barberà, Costers del Segre, Terra Alta, Priorat, Montsant and Tarragona—produce a remarkable number of fine wines. Highlights

include Miguel Torres, in Penedès; Castillo de Perelada in Costa Brava, for both sparkling and table wines; and D'Anguera and Capçanes in Montsant. The Priorat, a small, mountainous region full of ancient garnacha and cariñena vines, produces inky, powerful, rich reds; they're expensive wines, but extremely good. Names to look for include Alvaro Palacios, Mas Martinet and Clos Mogador.

The perfect finale to a Catalan meal is cremat, a hot coffee punch brought back from Cuba by Catalan colonizers. Spanish brandy, light rum and sugar are mixed in an earthenware bowl with lemon peel and a stick of cinnamon. The mixture is ignited, the alcohol allowed to burn off, and then hot black coffee and a few coffee beans are added. Cremat is traditionally accompanied by the singing of habaneras, sailors' songs named after the Cuban capital.

RECIPES

TORTILLA ESPAÑOLA (SPANISH OMELET)

This popular tapa is similar to an Italian frittata. Any number of ingredients can make their way into this omelet, depending on the season and/or region, though spinach and potato are the most classic fillings.

Serves 4

4	tbsp. extra-virgin olive oil
1	small yellow onion, peeled and chopped
2	cloves garlic, peeled and chopped
½	pound baby spinach
1	medium waxy potato, cooked, peeled and diced

Salt and freshly ground black pepper

8	eggs

1. Preheat oven to 325° F. Heat the oil in a medium non-stick skillet over medium-high heat. Add the onions and garlic and cook for 5 minutes. Add the spinach and cook, stirring often, until spinach liquid has rendered out and evaporated, about 10 minutes. Stir in the potatoes and season to taste with salt and pepper.

2. Whisk the eggs vigorously in a bowl until well beaten and aerated. Pour the eggs into the skillet and season with salt and pepper. Transfer skillet to the oven and bake until eggs are just set, about 20 minutes. Allow the omelet to cool for 10 minutes before inverting onto a plate. Serve at room temperature.

STUFFED PIQUILLO PEPPERS

Piquillo peppers are available in jars in most specialty food markets; the best are actually from Spain's Basque region.

Serves 4 to 6

½	pound best-quality salt cod
1	medium waxy potato, boiled, peeled and finely diced
½	cup plus 1 tbsp. extra-virgin olive oil

One 8-ounce jar whole Spanish piquillo peppers, drained

1. Soak the cod in a large bowl of water for 6 to 10 hours depending on the saltiness of the fish. Change the water every 3 to 4 hours. Bring a pot of water to a boil over high heat. Drain the cod and add it to the boiling water. Reduce heat to medium and simmer until fish begins to flake, about 10 minutes. Drain and transfer the fish to a work surface to let cool. Once cool enough to handle, remove any skin and bones and flake fish into small pieces. Transfer fish to the bowl of a standing mixer fitted with the paddle attachment. Beat the fish on medium speed until flakes are very small. Add the potato and beat until mixture is semi-smooth. With the motor running, slowly add ½ cup oil, beating until mixture is emulsified and light in texture.

2. Preheat oven to 350° F. Grease a medium baking dish with remaining oil and set aside. Spoon some of the salt cod puree into each piquillo pepper and transfer to the prepared dish. Cover dish with foil and bake until heated through, 10 to 15 minutes. Serve warm.

CHICKEN STUFFED WITH PRUNES

This wholesome dish is an example of Catalan regional cuisine, more from the hilly inland than the area directly around Barcelona.

Serves 4

6	tbsp. extra-virgin olive oil
½	small yellow onion, peeled and finely chopped
1	clove garlic, peeled and finely chopped
1½	cups pitted prunes
1	pinch Spanish paprika

Salt and freshly ground black pepper

4	boneless, skinless chicken breast halves
4	ounces semisoft Spanish goat's milk cheese, such as ibores or majorero
½	cup veal demi-glace
3	tbsp. Spanish sherry
¼	cup pine nuts, toasted

1. Heat 2 tbsp. oil in a small skillet over medium heat. Add the onions and garlic and cook until soft, about 5 minutes. Meanwhile, mince 1 cup prunes and transfer to a bowl. Add onions and garlic, paprika, and season to taste with salt and pepper. Stir until well mixed and set aside until cool.

2. Lay a chicken breast on a cutting board with the smooth side up and the pointed end facing away from you. Starting from the widest end, cut a deep pocket into the breast with a paring knife. Repeat the process with remaining breasts. Stuff each pocket with some of the cheese and 2 tbsp. of the prune filling. Skewer each opening shut with a toothpick and set aside.

3. Heat remaining oil in a large skillet over medium-high heat. Season the stuffed chicken with salt and pepper. Cook the chicken, turning once, until well browned all over, about 10 minutes. Add demi-glace and sherry, scraping up browned bits stuck to the bottom of the pan. Add remaining prunes, reduce heat to medium-low and simmer, partially covered, until chicken is cooked through, about 10 minutes. Season sauce to taste with salt and pepper.

4. Garnish each plate with pine nuts and prunes.

CANELONES
(SPANISH CANNELLONI)

*The pasta wrappers for this dish are smaller and thicker
than Italian cannelloni pasta and are typically made from
wheat starch and water, without any eggs. One great source
for them—and for any kind of Spanish foodstuff—
is www.tienda.com.*

Serves 4

3	tbsp. extra-virgin olive oil
1	small yellow onion, peeled and finely chopped
1	tomato, peeled, cored and finely chopped
2	cloves garlic, peeled and minced
¼	pound ground veal
¼	pound ground pork
¼	pound ground chicken or turkey, dark meat only
¼	tsp. dried thyme leaves

Pinch Spanish paprika

2	pinches freshly ground nutmeg

Salt and freshly ground black pepper

2	tbsp. fresh breadcrumbs
1	egg yolk, at room temperature
30	canelon wrappers
3	tbsp. plus ½ tsp. butter
2	tbsp. flour
1⅔	cups half-and-half
¼	cup freshly grated parmigiano-reggiano

1. Preheat oven to 350° F. Heat the oil in a skillet over medium heat. Add the onions, tomatoes and garlic and cook until onions are golden, 6 to 8 minutes. Add the veal, pork and chicken or turkey, increase heat to medium-high and cook until mixture begins to fry, about 10 minutes. Add the thyme, paprika, 1 pinch nutmeg, and season to taste with salt and pepper. Transfer the meat mixture to a bowl. Stir in the breadcrumbs and egg yolk and set aside to let cool.

2. Grease a medium baking dish with ½ tsp. butter and set aside. Bring a large pot of salted water to a boil. Working in small batches, add the canelon wrappers to the boiling water and cook, stirring often, until al dente, 6 to 8 minutes. Transfer wrappers with a slotted spoon to a clean dishtowel. Spoon 1 tbsp. of the meat filling on the bottom third of each square and roll wrapper up and over filling. Place filled canelones, seam side down, in the prepared dish. Repeat process with remaining wrappers and filling.

3. Melt the remaining butter in a saucepan over medium heat. Add the flour and stir constantly for 2 minutes. Gradually add the half-and-half and stir constantly until sauce thickens, about 5 minutes. Add the remaining nutmeg and season to taste with salt and pepper. Spoon the sauce over the canelones. Sprinkle the cheese over the sauce and bake until heated through, 10 to 15 minutes. If you like, brown the top under the broiler for 2 to 3 minutes.

ROMESCO

A good romesco is one of the basic ingredients of Catalan cooking, both as a condiment and an ingredient in various dishes.

Makes 1½ cups

1	ripe but firm tomato
3	dried medium-hot red chiles, such as ancho or New Mexico, stemmed and seeded
½	cup extra-virgin olive oil

One 1-inch-thick slice country bread

4 to 6 cloves garlic, crushed and peeled

¼	cup blanched almonds, toasted
¼	cup toasted unsalted hazelnuts, skinned

½ to 1 tsp. red wine vinegar

Salt

1. Preheat broiler. Roast the tomato about 3 inches from the flame, turning occasionally, until well charred and blistered all over, 8 to 10 minutes. Transfer the tomato to a bowl, cover and set aside for 5 minutes. Core, peel and seed tomato and set aside.

2. Heat a dry skillet over medium heat. Add the chiles and toast until fragrant, about 1 minute. Transfer chiles to a food processor and pulse until coarsely ground. Heat 2 tbsp. oil in the skillet over medium heat and toast bread until golden around the edges. Transfer bread to the food processor. Brown the garlic in the skillet and cook until lightly golden. Add the garlic, nuts and tomatoes to the food processor and pulse until finely ground. With the motor running, add the remaining oil in a slow steady stream and process until a chunky paste forms. Add the vinegar and season to taste with salt. Serve romesco with grilled meat, chicken, fish or vegetables, or use as a thick dressing for salad.

CREMA CATALANA (BURNT CRÈME CARAMEL)

The Catalan version of flan (or of crème brûlée, take your pick) is rich and sinfully delicious.

Serves 4

3	cups plus 1 tbsp. half-and-half

Three 1-inch-wide strips lemon peel

1	cinnamon stick
2	tbsp. cornstarch
9	egg yolks
13	tbsp. sugar

1. Preheat oven to 200° F. Bring 3 cups half-and-half, lemon peel and cinnamon stick to just a boil in a heavy saucepan over medium-high heat. Remove saucepan from the heat, cover and set aside to let steep for 10 minutes.

2. Whisk the cornstarch and remaining half-and-half together in a medium bowl. Add the egg yolks and 9 tbsp. sugar and whisk vigorously until thick and pale yellow. Slowly add 1 cup of the warm half-and-half, stirring constantly, and return the entire mixture to the saucepan. Heat over medium-low heat, stirring constantly with a wooden spoon, until thickened, 8 to 10 minutes.

3. Strain the custard through a fine sieve into a bowl, discarding solids. Divide custard between four 6-ounce cazuelas or other shallow ovenproof dishes. Cover each with foil and bake until custard is just set, 45 to 60 minutes. Sprinkle remaining sugar over each custard and broil 2 inches above the flame until sugar is caramelized, 2 to 4 minutes. Serve warm or at room temperature.

MOROCCO

*In Fez and in Marrakech,
the scent of the souks,
the allure of the medina*

LUNCH
UNDER A
BERBER TENT

DINNER AT
THE RESTAURANT
EL YACOUT

Morocco is the vivid beauty of the spice vendor's mounds of turmeric and saffron contrasted against the raw smell of the tannery nearby. It is the olive vendor's bowls of olives, flavored with citrus and glossy with oil, played against the ragged children begging for coins as you leave the market stall. Morocco is beautiful and complicated all at once — but isn't that always true of real beauty?

THE MOROCCAN LANDSCAPE

THOUGH THE STORIES YOU'VE HEARD may make Morocco seem like a desert, in truth the country is fertile and alive. The long coastline meanders for hundreds of miles, and inland lie plains that for centuries have produced a cornucopia of citrus fruits, vegetables and grains. Only far to the east in the shadow of the Atlas and Rif mountain ranges do the fields turn barren; and far to the south, where the Sahara parches the soil to sand, and water becomes as valuable as gold.

But whatever the character of the Moroccan countryside, the cities are the magnets that pull people from all corners of the country. Casablanca and Rabat, Fez and Marrakech—these are the vibrant centers of this alluring nation. Here thousands upon thousands of people navigate the narrow, winding streets, heed the voice of the muezzin calling them to prayer throughout the course of the day, pause at one of the myriad shops selling anything imaginable. Veiled women moving like whispers, men in their hooded djellabas, careless boys racing past, dodging between the laden donkeys—Morocco is as dense and varied as a symphony, especially in Marrakech's Jamaa El F'na square, home to snake charmers, storytellers and jugglers. By twilight, though, the food sellers have set up their stalls. Everyone enjoys the cool of the evening, stopping for a bite of this and a bite of that, until full night falls.

LUNCH
UNDER A
BERBER TENT

THIS WAS THE PERFECT SETTING for our lunch, a Berber tent on a horse farm outside Marrakech. The farm itself was gorgeous, a true oasis in the midst of the desert—we drove up amid date palms to stone walls over which scarlet bougainvillea poured, and inside the walls everything was lush, green, saturated.

The tent itself was perfect, but there was nothing under it! Thinking quickly, I asked the farm's owner to bring out a short table or two, wooden frames on top of which we set Berber cushions and a rich variety of Berber rugs. In Marrakech I had already purchased dozens of lamps of every size and shape, with intricate metalwork and blue and green glass faces, three or four at each corner of the tent and more on the table. Bowls of fruit, a giant platter of couscous and a seemingly infinite array of Moroccan salads completed the scene.

CREATING A MOROCCAN TABLE

WITH THESE PLACE SETTINGS I worked to capture the rich textures and colors of Morocco, placing different patterns one atop another in a kind of layering effect. The dishes themselves were from the medina in Fez, and the glasses are Moroccan tea glasses. I chose them in blue and green to complement the lanterns, but they're available in many other colors as well in the markets of Marrakech.

I used a Berber rug from the Atlas Mountains for the tablecloth, with a gold wool shawl as a second layer on top; it, too, is of Berber origin, worn against the mountain cold and embedded with sparkly bits of metal on one side, similar to the napkins with their decorative metal bangles.

All of the food was homemade, small dishes of the savory salads the Moroccans serve at every meal, like the delicious fava bean salad pictured at left. Of course, serving so many different snacks all at the same time, each in differently patterned bowls, adds to that exotic layering quality I worked to establish here.

Mounds of yellow and red spices recall the markets in Fez and Marrakech, while a chicken tagine served on a bed of couscous is quintessentially Moroccan. Bowls of tropical fruit carry the color theme a step farther, their red and gold echoing the shades of the wool shawls used as tablecloths.

DINNER AT THE RESTAURANT EL YACOUT

AN ARABIAN NIGHTS FANTASY, Restaurant El Yacout in Marrakech may well be the world's most romantic restaurant. To heighten the romance—if such a thing is possible!—I strewed the floor with thousands of rose petals in white, pink, red and yellow, then created a rose "snake," made of rosebuds wrapped around a frame of chicken wire, to slither seductively from table to floor.

A ring of rosebuds surrounded each plate, too, which was set atop a patterned metal grate (actually used for windows). The fanciful blue bowls are in fact traditional tagine bowls—though I suppose it's very untraditional to serve rose petals in them. For napkin rings, a bit of two-inch tapestry trim did the trick. The centerpiece, from the market in Marrakech, is made of black glass and metal, and anchors the setting beautifully.

FOODS OF MOROCCO

MOROCCAN CUISINE is rich and heavily spiced, though not fiercely so (the way a Thai curry might be, for instance). Most dishes are of Berber origin, but the Arabs and the French each added their own touches through the years, and the result is one of the most indulgent and complex cuisines in the world.

Meals often start with *harira*, a thick soup whose character varies from place to place—typically, though, it's made with lamb, lentils, tomatoes, onion, garlic and spices, and is always served with bread. Main courses include couscous, traditionally made of coarsely ground wheat but nowadays more likely to consist of grains of semolina pasta, served either way with vegetables and sometimes meat; *tagine*, a stew of vegetables and meat flavored with olives, preserved lemons, garlic, cumin, ginger, saffron and turmeric; *mechoui*, or roasted lamb; and *b'steeya*, which is phyllo dough molded around shredded pigeon or chicken, ground almonds and spices, baked and sprinkled with powdered sugar and cinnamon (it's quite rich). Of course, for the ingredients for all these dishes, you'll have to head to Morocco's abundant souks, or markets.

(continued on page 177)

Olives are a staple in Morocco, found in every marketplace, mounded high and glistening with oil. Moroccan bread is flat, with a soft crust and a dense, spongy interior. It's ideal for sopping up the sauce of a savory tagine or even as your main utensil, if you're eating Moroccan-style.

(continued from page 174)

VEGETABLES AND FRUITS

The souk is an abundant source of fruits and vegetables. In season, Morocco's tomatoes are among the world's finest; look also for beets, carrots, eggplants, onions, fava beans, zucchini, parsley and mint (for mint tea, of course). As for fruit, you'll see oranges, lemons, pomegranates, prickly pears, nectarines, peaches, strawberries and a cornucopia of dried fruit (including the best dried apricots you're ever likely to taste). Salt-preserved lemons are a key condiment in Moroccan cuisine, used to flavor stews and tagines and sold in the souks either loose or in jars.

GRAINS, SEEDS AND NUTS

As the Moroccan saying has it, "each grain of couscous represents a good deed." Standard couscous is formed of small grains of durum wheat semolina (essentially a grainlike pasta). Hull-less cracked barley, known as belboula, is the basic ingredient in barley couscous, an interesting alternative to the standard variety. Other popular items in Moroccan markets include sesame seeds—sold hulled and unhulled and used in breads and pastries—as well as an abundance of almonds, walnuts, peanuts and pine nuts.

OLIVES AND OLIVE OIL

Phoenician traders introduced olives to North Africa more than five thousand years ago, and they are essential to Moroccan cuisine. In the markets, vendors sell a dazzling array of olives: green, purple and black olives, water- or brine-cured, sometimes combined with dried herbs, chiles or preserved lemon. (Look for the violet-colored ones preserved with the juice of bitter oranges for an unusual delight.) You'll also find abundant Moroccan olive oil, soft and fruity, another essential ingredient.

SPICES AND SEASONINGS

Morocco's cuisine is based on complex blends of spices, and it's no surprise that spice vendors abound in the markets, often simply presenting their wares in enormous colorful mounds. Cumin, ground ginger, saffron, turmeric, paprika and orange blossoms turn the market stalls into washes of pure color. And each vendor will often have his or her own version of ras el hanout, the traditional Moroccan spice blend (the name translates to "top of the shop"). As many as thirty or forty ingredients may enter into ras el hanout, but several common ones are the above-mentioned spices, plus allspice, nutmeg, black pepper, mace and cinnamon. Also investigate tinctures like rose water, made by steam-distilling rose oil obtained from damask roses, and orange-flower water, which is also used extensively in Moroccan baking. It's distilled from the blossoms of the Seville orange tree, and is lightly bitter and tropical all at once.

PASTRIES

Moroccans love sweet baked items, pastries and desserts, often filled with ground nuts, dates or figs, flavored with rose- or orange-blossom water, and saturated with honey. Some sweets to look for are briouats, triangular pastries that have been dipped in simmering honey; ktaif, sheets of pastry fried in butter, spread with an almond and cinnamon mixture, and flavored with orange-flower water; kaab el ghazal, pastries filled with almond paste and formed to look like gazelle's horns; and m'hancha, a flat, round pastry stuffed with almonds and coated with icing and cinnamon.

WINES OF MOROCCO

While most Moroccans are adherents of Islam, a religion that forbids the consumption of alcohol, the country was a French protectorate for many years and consequently has a lengthy history of wine production; it even has a quality classification system similar to the French appellation contrôlée. Morocco produces mostly red wines, and while the bulk of them are exported to Europe for blending, there are some appealing wines available domestically. Typically they're rustic and full-flavored, without much elegance but with a warm-climate richness that can be pleasant with the country's highly spiced cuisine. The main vineyard areas are located near Casablanca and Rabat on the coast and inland near Meknes and Fez; the most widely planted grape varieties are, unsurprisingly, French: alicante bouschet, carignan, cinsault, grenache, syrah and a little mourvèdre. A few brands worth looking for include Ksar, Amazir, Guerrouane, Baraka and Sidi Brahim. Note, though, that in many restaurants in Morocco it may be difficult to find wines at all, because of Islamic restrictions.

MOROCCAN MINT TEA

ماء الورد

MINT TEA IS SERVED at all times and for all occasions in Morocco. It appears at every meal, but also at midday in teashops, where Moroccans gather to discuss, it seems, every topic under the sun, and it's essential in the marketplace, whether to greet a potential customer or to seal a deal. In fact, it's not unusual to see a local shop owner and customer bargaining with such ferocity that it seems they're about to go for one another's throats, only to have them suddenly agree on a price and then sit down to a cup of mint tea.

Served in small glass cups filled half-full, and often poured from a great height in a steaming aromatic stream, Moroccan mint tea fills the room with its scent. Traditionally it's made from green gunpowder tea, sprigs of fresh mint and huge amounts of sugar.

MINT TEA

Serves 2

2	tbsp. green tea, such as gunpowder
4 to 6	tbsp. sugar
½	bunch mint, trimmed

Steep the tea and 3 cups boiling water together for 3 to 4 minutes. Put the sugar and mint into a teapot. Strain the hot tea over the sugar and mint and stir until sugar dissolves.

MARKETS
OF MOROCCO

THE SYMPHONY OF MOROCCO reaches its crescendo in the old towns of Fez and Marrakech. Everything here is negotiable. In fact, a Moroccan merchant would probably be appalled by a shopper who simply paid the asking price without complaint (not that that would stop him from taking the money!). That's because trade is a social activity here, thousands of miles and years divorced from our antiseptic shelves and pasted-on price stickers. After all, when was the last time you were offered a glass of mint tea after paying for your purchases at an American supermarket?

FEZ

Visiting the market in Fez is like stepping back into Biblical times. Miles of winding streets turn and twist upon one another and you soon lose all sense of direction. The streets are so narrow that only donkeys can go in and out, no cars or trucks, and they're crammed with shops, organized into souks—areas that specialize in a certain product.

Down one alley, woodworkers are bent to the task, pumping the wheels of their foot-powered lathes; down another, piles of multicolored spices glow in orange and red, yellow and black. Turn a corner and raw wool lies in piles; turn another and heaps of carpets await your ability to bargain. You hear the banging of the metalworkers' mallets and smell the ripe and overpowering odor of the ancient tannery. This is truly a glimpse of a timeless Morocco, seemingly no different than it must have been five hundred years ago.

MARRAKECH

The market in Marrakech is more modern than that of Fez, partly owing to Marrakech's enormous popularity as a tourist destination in recent years. The space is more open, too, which allows motorcycles, cars and small trucks to navigate the streets—though donkeys plod along here too, just as in Fez. Both cities offer many of the same products for sale, although you're likely to find some slightly trendier items in Marrakech. And because Marrakech is closer to Berber territory, you'll see more Berbers in their traditional blue clothing on the streets of the city and an assortment of Berber textiles, shawls, rugs and pottery in market stalls. In the center of the kaleidescope that is Marrakech is its fabled town square, Jemaa El F'na, a round-the-clock performance space filled with storytellers, jugglers, snake charmers, fortune tellers and other "only-in-Marrakech" characters.

Atlantic Ocean

Tangier

Rabat

Casablanca

Fez

Meknes

Marrakech

Agadir

RECIPES

MOROCCAN MEALS almost always start with an array of salads. These are typically small plates of cooked vegetables, spiced and served in olive oil. On this page is a trio of classic Moroccan salad recipes. Another simple and delicious choice is the traditional fava bean salad—simply cook a cup and a half of fava beans in boiling salted water for about two and a half minutes, and drain. Season the beans with a tablespoon of olive oil, two tablespoons of chopped preserved lemon peel, some chopped parsley and a touch of salt.

EGGPLANT SALAD

Serves 6

1	medium globe eggplant, trimmed, peeled and cubed
Salt	
4	tbsp. olive oil
2	ripe red tomatoes, peeled, cored, seeded and chopped
2	cloves garlic, peeled and minced
Leaves from 6 sprigs cilantro, finely chopped	
¼	tsp. ground cumin
¼	tsp. smoked paprika

Toss the eggplant and 1 tbsp. salt together in a bowl. Set aside for 20 minutes. Squeeze juices out of eggplant with a clean kitchen towel. Heat the oil in a skillet over high heat. Add eggplants and fry until golden, 6 to 8 minutes. Using a slotted spoon, transfer eggplants to a food processor and puree. Return puree to skillet on medium heat. Add the tomatoes, garlic, cilantro, cumin and paprika, season to taste with salt and cook until very thick and oil separates from mixture, 15 to 20 minutes. Serve at room temperature.

BEET SALAD

Serves 6

1½	pounds beets, greens trimmed
Salt	
1	tbsp. fresh lemon juice
1	tbsp. olive oil
1	tsp. sugar
⅛	tsp. paprika
Pinch ground cinnamon	

1. Boil beets in a pot of salted water until tender, 25 to 30 minutes. Drain and peel beets then cut into ¼-inch cubes.

2. Whisk the lemon juice, olive oil, sugar, paprika and cinnamon together in a bowl. Add the beets, toss and let marinate 1 hour.

RED AND GREEN TOMATO SALAD

Serves 6

1	tbsp. olive oil
1	tsp. fresh lemon juice
1	clove garlic, minced
1	tbsp. chopped fresh parsley leaves
1	tbsp. chopped fresh cilantro leaves
½	tsp. chopped fresh marjoram leaves
¼	tsp. ground cumin
2	ripe red tomatoes, cored, seeded and diced
2	green tomatoes, cored, seeded and diced
Salt	

Whisk the oil, lemon juice, garlic, parsley, cilantro, marjoram and cumin together in a bowl. Add the tomatoes, season with salt, toss and let marinate 1 hour.

SEVEN-VEGETABLE COUSCOUS

Couscous, Morocco's national dish, can be served many ways—but if you really want to follow Moroccan tradition, try eating your couscous with the first three fingers of your right hand.

Serves 6

2½   cups standard couscous (not instant)

5   cups chicken stock

2   ripe tomatoes, peeled, seeded and quartered

1   medium yellow onion, peeled and cut into sixths

1   stick cinnamon

Leaves from 3 sprigs cilantro, chopped

Leaves from 3 sprigs parsley, chopped

⅛   tsp. ground turmeric

Pinch saffron

6   tbsp. butter

3   medium carrots, peeled, halved lengthwise
       and cut into 1-inch pieces

2   medium turnips, peeled and cut into
       1-inch pieces

1   small squash, such as butternut or acorn,
       peeled, seeded and cut into 1-inch pieces

Salt and freshly ground black pepper

2   zucchini, trimmed, quartered lengthwise
       and cut into 1-inch pieces

¼   cup raisins

1½   cups cooked chickpeas, rinsed and drained

¼   cup harissa (Moroccan hot pepper paste)

I. Rinse the couscous in a large bowl of cold water. Drain and spread couscous out on a baking sheet and set aside to let hydrate for 10 minutes. Put the stock, tomatoes, onions, cinnamon stick, cilantro, parsley, turmeric, saffron and half of the butter into the bottom pot of a couscousier and bring to a boil over medium-high heat. Reduce heat to low, cover and simmer until onions are very soft, 40 to 50 minutes.

2. Lightly rub the couscous between the palms of your hands to remove any lumps. Sprinkle the couscous in the top steamer pot of the couscousier into a mound. This will prevent the couscous from lumping together. Place the top steamer pot on top of the bottom pot. Cover the top pot and steam for 20 minutes. Add the carrots, turnips and squash to the bottom pot, season to taste with salt and pepper and simmer until vegetables are cooked through, about 15 minutes. Add the zucchini, raisins and chickpeas and simmer 10 minutes more. Continue steaming the couscous while the vegetables simmer.

3. Pour the steamed couscous into a serving dish, add the remaining butter and toss until butter is completely melted. Remove and discard the cinnamon stick. Using a slotted spoon, lift the vegetables and chickpeas from the pot and arrange on top of the couscous. Adjust the broth for seasonings and moisten the couscous with some of the broth. Serve with harissa on the side.

CHICKEN WITH BLACK OLIVES
AND PRESERVED LEMONS

*Preserved lemons are available in jars at many gourmet shops
and Middle Eastern groceries.*

Serves 6

5	cloves garlic, peeled and chopped
¾	tsp. paprika
¾	tsp. ground cumin
¼	tsp. ground ginger
¼	tsp. ground turmeric
Salt	
4	tbsp. olive oil
1	tbsp. fresh lemon juice
1	large yellow onion, peeled and grated on the holes of a box grater

One 4- to 5-pound whole chicken, cut into 12 pieces

2	pinches saffron

Leaves from 4 sprigs cilantro, chopped

Leaves from 4 sprigs parsley, chopped

1	preserved lemon, rinsed
¾	cup cured black olives, pitted

1. Pound the garlic, paprika, cumin, ginger, turmeric, 1 tsp. salt, oil, lemon juice and one quarter of the onions together in a mortar and pestle to a semi-smooth paste. Transfer the paste to a large glass bowl. Add the chicken pieces and rub the marinade into the chicken until well coated. Cover with plastic wrap and refrigerate overnight.

2. The following day, put the chicken and marinade into a heavy medium-size pot. Cover and heat over medium heat. Stir the saffron into ¼ cup warm water and add it to the pot. Add the cilantro, parsley and remaining onions and season to taste with salt. Simmer, partially covered and stirring occasionally, until chicken is cooked through, 50 to 60 minutes.

3. Remove and discard the pulp from the preserved lemon. Chop the rind and add it to the pot. Stir in olives and simmer 10 minutes more. Adjust seasonings before serving.

LAMB TAGINE WITH HONEY

Though this sounds sweet, it isn't—just savory and delicious, with a light edge of sweetness to play against the spice of the ginger and ras el hanout.

Serves 6

2	cups pitted prunes
2	tbsp. olive oil
4	tbsp. butter
4	cloves garlic, peeled and thinly sliced
1½	tsp. ras el hanout (Moroccan spice mixture)
¼	tsp. ground ginger
⅛	tsp. cayenne

Pinch ground saffron

1	small cinnamon stick
3	pounds lamb shoulder, trimmed of excess fat and cut into large pieces
½	cup finely ground almonds
1	small yellow onion, peeled and finely chopped

Leaves from 8 sprigs cilantro, chopped

Leaves from 8 sprigs parsley, chopped

Salt and freshly ground black pepper

4	tbsp. honey

1. Finely chop half of the prunes and set aside. Heat the oil and butter in a tagine or wide, heavy, medium-size pot over medium heat. Add the garlic, ras el hanout, ginger, cayenne, saffron and cinnamon stick and cook until garlic is no longer raw. Add the lamb, almonds, half of the onions, half of the cilantro and parsley, the chopped prunes and 1½ cups water. Season to taste with salt and pepper. Reduce heat to low, cover and simmer, stirring occasionally, until meat is tender, about 1 hour.

2. Add the honey and the remaining onions, cilantro, parsley and whole prunes. Simmer, partially covered, until meat is very tender, about 1 hour more. Transfer the meat and prunes to a warm plate and cover to keep warm. Increase the heat to medium and boil the sauce, stirring often, until very thick and mahogany brown, 20 to 25 minutes. Adjust the seasonings. Return the meat and prunes to the sauce and cook until warmed through.

NETHERLANDS

*A swirl of colorful petals
rises against the gray line
of the ever-present sea*

COCKTAILS
AND
DINNER
IN A
TULIP FIELD

In the Netherlands, the boundary between land and sea can seem illusory. Yet salt water could never yield such a floral abundance. Walk a few steps in from the waterline and take a seat in a field of tulips. Van Gogh may have lived in France, but he was a true Dutchman; one glance at these blooms explains his amazing eye for color.

THE DUTCH LANDSCAPE

THE NETHERLANDS IS DEFINED and shaped by water. Its story is largely that of a nation's courage and ingenuity in wresting the land back from the ever-encroaching sea.

Even if you're not within sight of the coast, you sense the omnipresence of water here—in the soft air and saturated ground, in the amazing fecundity of the tulip fields, in Amsterdam with its canals and the countryside with its dikes and marshes. And while the landscape of the Netherlands can be dour, especially during the cold winter months (or when you're desperately hoping for the sun to peek out during a photo shoot, as I was!), it is also immensely beautiful, with its low skies and gentle pastures; its rich, glowing light captured so famously by Rembrandt and Vermeer; and those endless, ordered rows of tulips stretching like paint strokes into a hazy distance. (The field pictured here is just a few short miles outside Amsterdam's city limits.)

More tulips are grown in the Netherlands than anywhere else on Earth, and more flowers in general are grown here than in many countries ten times its size, but there's something about the tulip—its neatly ordered petals, straight green stem and scentless modesty—that epitomizes the beauty and restraint of this water-bound land.

COCKTAILS AND DINNER IN A TULIP FIELD

THE IDEA FOR THIS BOOK actually came to me while I was standing in a radiant field of tulips, a few miles north of Amsterdam. Up until that moment, the weather in Holland had been unseasonably cold and gloomy, but it had broken that morning, and now the sun appeared. The tulips—pink, red, yellow, white— stretched in unbroken rows into the distance, the blooms seeming to raise their petals to the emergent sun.

This was exactly what I had envisioned for our cocktail-and-dinner party, a kind of floral dreamscape stretching away in every direction around a group of people laughing and enjoying sips of Dutch genever and intriguing hors d'oeuvres, then sitting down for a traditional Dutch dinner in a sea of red flowers.

For this cocktail party in the flowers, I used galvanized watering cans as vases, filled with tulips. The wickerwork chairs evoke Holland's colonial past, while the pairs of clogs on each cocktail table, filled with more tulips, are a whimsical nod to one of the country's national symbols. A selection of Dutch beers and genevers is offered, along with crudités fresh from the Amsterdam markets.

CREATING A
DUTCH TABLE

I GOT VERY LUCKY with this table, because the light in the Netherlands can be capricious—one moment dark and stormy, the next moment golden and glowing. Of course, I wanted the latter, and I'm still amazed that on the one afternoon we had to shoot, I got it.

For this dinner, I covered the table with a Battenberg lace tablecloth over a multicolored pastel dupioni silk underlay. A floral centerpiece seemed de rigueur for a meal amidst the flowers. Although initially we tried using many different types of flowers, in the end I decided to take everything out except the tulips—with a few sprays of white for contrast. The centerpiece was a moss-covered wicker basket that matched the high-backed wickerwork chairs. The brightly colored flatware, resting on a bed of moss, repeated the tulip motif in its pattern.

We arranged gerber daisies or bunches of tulips on the seats of the chairs—of course, you'd want to move them before you sat down! And since we were in the middle of a field, I covered the place settings with light mesh domes, somewhat as a lark, but I liked the whimsical feel it gave to the whole affair.

For our tulip-field dinner, I used single tulip leaves as napkin rings, knotting them loosely but carefully. The chargers are made of galvanized tin, while the plates are decorated with butterflies and bees. Each place setting features a small gift—an individual pot displaying one particular type of flower.

FOODS OF THE NETHERLANDS

THE DUTCH aren't really known for their cuisine, but the traditional dishes of the Netherlands do have their appealing characteristics. They tend to be hearty, sustaining and simple—good fare on a cold winter night after a long day of work—with stews and soups taking a primary role. Some classic Dutch dishes include *stamppot*, a mix of mashed potatoes and various vegetables, often served with sausages or braised meats; *erwtensoep*, a thick, creamy pea soup full of winter vegetables and chunks of bacon or ham; *rolpens met hatebliksem*, or sausages made with a mixture of minced tripe, beef and pork, served with a mashed apple-and-potato mixture; *hazepeper*, which is rabbit marinated in vinegar and wine and then stewed; *krabbetjes*, which are Dutch beef spareribs, cooked until they're meltingly tender; and *uitsmijter*, which is essentially ham and eggs, but covered in melted cheese. In fact, perhaps hearty is an understatement for this very filling cuisine!

FISH

There are many kinds of fresh fish available in the Netherlands, but the real excitement belongs to the humble herring. The Dutch love herring, and each May herring fever hits the country as the Dutch devour Hollandse nieuwe, *or first-of-the-season herring. Typically the fish is served raw with chopped onion and pickles, but it may be best eaten by itself. The "green" herring, as they are also known, are so rich and full of flavor that the condiments only seem to get in the way.*

CHEESE

The Dutch produce several superb cheeses, and the commercial cheese market in Alkmaar, with its porters in their white uniforms and straw hats, is one of the country's many tourist attractions. The best-known Dutch cheeses are all made from cow's milk and include boerenkaas, *a fresh farmer's cheese made from unpasteurized milk;* nagelkaas, *or nail-cheese, so named for the appearance of the cloves it's flavored with;* gouda, *with its nutty, rich flavor;* edam, *which is mild and creamy; and* leiden, *which is flavored with cumin seeds.*

RIJSTTAFEL

The best-loved meal in the Netherlands doesn't originate here at all, but rather in Indonesia, one of the former colonies (and where, in fact, it's rarely served anymore). A rijsttafel, or rice table, consists of plain white rice served along with several—up to twenty or thirty—side dishes of meat, fish, chicken, vegetables and condiments. This seems like a vast amount of food, but the idea really is to taste as many different dishes as possible, rather than to fill up on any one item. Classic rijsttafel components include satay, *or pork kebabs served with peanut sauce;* gado-gado, *vegetables in a similar peanut sauce;* kroepoek, *which are small shrimp toasts;* perkedel, *or potato-and-meat fritters;* kari ikan, *or fish curry; and many others.*

PASTRIES

The Netherlands produces an abundance of sweet baked goods, such as speculaas, *a much-loved spicy Dutch cookie flavored with cinnamon, nutmeg and cloves;* boterkoek, *an almond butter cake, made from torte pastry with an almond filling flavored with honey;* ollibollen, *a kind of doughnut usually sprinkled with powdered sugar;* poffertjes, *which are silver-dollar-sized pancakes served with melted butter and powdered sugar; and* appelflappen, *or deep-fried apple fritters.*

MARKETS OF AMSTERDAM

THE NETHERLANDS has a long history as a great trading nation, and the markets of Amsterdam bear witness to the commercial prowess of the Dutch. Probably the most famous market in the city is the Albert Cuypmarkt, located in the De Pijp district. Over three hundred stalls sell goods of all kinds; everything from an enormous variety of foodstuffs, both Dutch and foreign, to clothes, flowers and knickknacks.

Another of Amsterdam's famous markets is the picturesque Noordemarkt. Most days it's a general market offering a variety of goods, but on Saturdays, it turns into a bird market and a farmers' market specializing in organic fruits, vegetables and herbs. On Mondays, it features a popular flea market.

Other Amsterdam markets focus on specific products. The city's renowned Bloemenmarkt ("flower market"), for example, is a collection of barges on the Singel canal ablaze with colorful blooms—tulips for the most part, of course, but also many other types of flowers as well. With more than fifty thousand acres

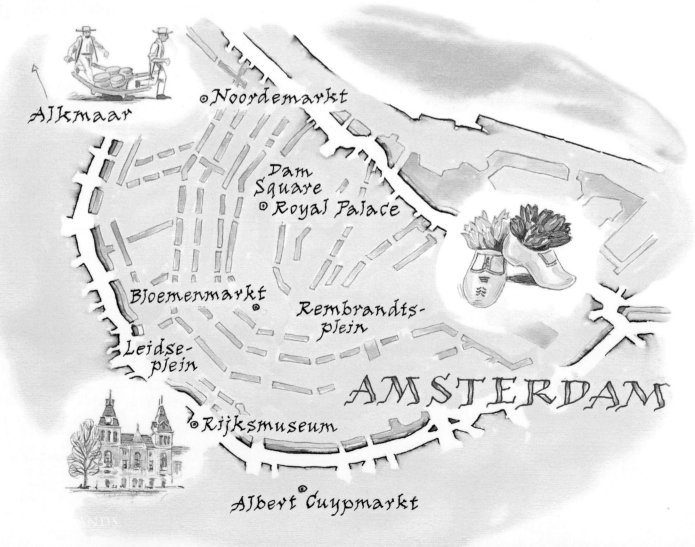

Alkmaar

Noordemarkt

Dam Square

Royal Palace

Bloemenmarkt

Rembrandts-plein

Leidse-plein

Rijksmuseum

AMSTERDAM

Albert Cuypmarkt

of this small country's surface area given over to the production of bulbs, there are more than enough flowers here to go around.

If you're visiting Holland in the summer, don't miss the picturesque cheese markets in the towns of Alkmaar and Gouda. In Alkmaar, porters in white costumes and straw hats race about with wooden barrows full of cheese slung from their shoulders. Buyers and sellers trade furiously, with the buyers occasionally indulging in the time-honored ritual of "cheese bashing," or smacking a cheese with the palm of the hand to determine its firmness and quality.

A must-see for any amateur gardener, the Aalsmeer Flower Auction is held in an enormous building outside Amsterdam. Every day more than twenty million flowers and plants from more than seven thousand different growers are sold here. Believe it or not, if you buy a tulip on Tuesday morning in Little Rock, Arkansas, there's a good chance it was shipped from the Aalsmeer Flower Auction just a day or two before.

GENEVER AND DUTCH BEER

THE DUTCH CERTAINLY drink wine, but the climate of the Netherlands isn't suited to its production. Instead—and to our great benefit—the Dutch produce gin, known in Holland as *genever*, and beer. Gin, or genever, is thought to have been invented around 1650 by a Dutch physician named Dr. Sylvius. His original intent was to create a cure for kidney ailments—little did he know what he was starting.

Dutch genever is slightly different from the better-known English style of gin. It's thicker in texture, has a yellowish color, and is more strongly flavored with juniper (the dominant flavor note in almost all gin). And in the Netherlands it's almost always drunk neat, often icy cold, rather than in mixed drinks.

Of course, the Dutch also love beer. Heineken's former main brewery is located in Amsterdam and still offers tours; Amstel and Grolsch are also well-known names. If you're feeling adventurous, though, try a glass of *oud bruin*, or old brown, a dark, mild beer that's low in alcohol and sweetened with natural sugar; it is a style, rather than a brand, and most of the major brewers sell a version of it.

RECITES

FINGER SANDWICHES WITH THREE SPREADS

You'll find gouda aged anywhere from six months to seven years—the older it is, though, the more nutty and sharp the flavor will be.

Serves 2 to 4

1	cup cream cheese, at room temperature
1	cup finely grated aged gouda
2	tsp. dijon mustard
¼	tsp. paprika
⅛	tsp. cayenne
¼	cup minced watercress leaves

Salt and freshly ground black pepper

8	square slices Dutch rye bread

1. Put ⅓ cup cream cheese and ⅓ cup gouda into a small bowl. Add the dijon mustard, season to taste with salt and pepper and stir until well mixed. Set mustard spread aside. Repeat the process two more times, making a paprika-and-cayenne spread and a watercress spread. Divide the mustard spread between two slices of rye, spreading out to an even layer. Place another two slices of rye on top and spread with the paprika-and-cayenne mixture. Repeat the process with the watercress mixture and top with the remaining rye, making two stacked sandwiches, each with three layers of spread. Gently press down layers to compact. Using a serrated knife, trim off the crusts then cut each sandwich into quarters.

PICKLED HERRING OVER BEET SALAD

This traditional Dutch dish can be an alarming shade of purple, but it's very tasty.

Makes about 40

2	medium beets, trimmed, cooked, peeled and coarsely chopped
5	cornichons, drained
1	tbsp. capers, drained
2	tsp. dijon mustard

Leaves from 3 sprigs parsley

1	tbsp. lemon juice

Salt and freshly ground black pepper

One 600-gram bottle pickled herring, drained

8	heads Belgian endive, leaves separated

1. Put the beets, cornichons, capers, dijon mustard, parsley, lemon juice and salt and pepper to taste into a food processor and pulse until finely chopped but not mushy. Set the beet salad aside.

2. Cut the herring into 1-inch squares and set aside. Spoon 2 tsp. of the beet salad on the root end of each endive leaf and top each with a square of herring. Serve chilled.

SAUSAGE IN PUFF PASTRY

A variation on saucijzenbrood, *which itself is essentially a Dutch variation on the hotdog.*

Makes about 24

½   pound store-bought puff pastry, thawed

Flour

½   pound loose sausage meat

1   egg, beaten

1. Preheat oven to 400° F. Line a baking sheet with parchment paper or aluminum foil and set aside.

2. Roll the puff pastry out on a lightly floured work surface to about ¼-inch thickness. Using a sharp knife cut the pastry into 2½-inch-wide strips. Cut each strip crosswise in 2½-inch intervals to make squares. Put about ½ tsp. of the sausage meat in the center of each square. Fold two sides of pastry towards each other, slightly overlapping and covering meat. Gently press down on open ends and trim off excess with a knife. Brush tops with some of the egg then transfer to the prepared baking sheet and refrigerate for 10 minutes.

3. Bake pastries until golden brown and meat is fully cooked through, about 15 minutes. Transfer pastries to a serving platter and serve immediately.

DUTCH SPLIT PEA SOUP

Otherwise known as erwtensoep, *this is a very filling soup— it can easily work as a meal by itself.*

Serves 4

1½   cups split green peas

4   slices bacon, coarsely chopped

2   cups veal or chicken stock

1   small yellow onion, peeled and chopped

1   leek, white and pale green part only, chopped

½   small celery root, peeled and chopped

Salt and freshly ground black pepper

16   slices smoked sausage

1   scallion, trimmed and chopped

2   tbsp. heavy cream

1. Soak the peas in a large bowl of water for 2 to 3 hours. Drain and transfer to a medium pot. Add the bacon, stock and 2 cups water and bring to a boil over high heat. Stir in the onions, leeks and celery root and season to taste with salt and pepper. Reduce heat to medium-low and simmer, partially covered, until peas and vegetables are very tender, about 1½ hours.

2. Working in batches, puree the soup in a blender. Transfer puree to a clean pot and heat over medium until hot. Garnish with some of the sausages, scallions and heavy cream.

RED CABBAGE

Cabbage turns up in many traditional Dutch dishes, but it's also delicious as a side dish, seasoned to have a touch of sweetness.

Serves 4

2	whole cloves
1	bay leaf

One 1-inch-wide strip orange peel

1	cinnamon stick
1	small head red cabbage, halved, cored and thinly sliced
3	tbsp. red currant jelly
2	tbsp. brown sugar
1	tbsp. uncooked rice
¼	cup orange juice
¼	cup red wine
2	tsp. butter

Salt

1. Put the cloves, bay leaf, orange peel and cinnamon stick into the center of a piece of cheesecloth. Gather the corners together and tie shut with kitchen twine. Set the sachet aside.

2. Put the cabbage, jelly, sugar, rice, orange juice, wine, butter, ¼ cup water, sachet and salt to taste into a medium pot. Bring to a boil over medium-high heat and cook, stirring occasionally, until cabbage is completely wilted, 6 to 8 minutes. Reduce heat to medium-low and cook, partially covered, until cabbage is very soft, about 1 hour. Remove the sachet before serving. Serve alongside grilled sausages and vegetable mashed potatoes.

STAMPPOT (VEGETABLE MASHED POTATOES)

This version of a Dutch classic is prepared with kale and carrots. In the Netherlands, kale is considered best when harvested after the first frost.

Serves 4

4	russet potatoes

Salt

8	tbsp. butter
2	kale leaves, center rib and stem removed and leaf finely chopped
1	small carrot, peeled and finely chopped
1	small yellow onion, peeled and finely chopped

Freshly ground white pepper

6	tbsp. milk

1. Put the potatoes into a medium pot and cover with salted water by 2 inches. Bring to a boil over medium-high heat and cook until potatoes are tender, about 30 minutes.

2. Meanwhile, heat 3 tbsp. butter in a skillet over medium heat. Add the kale, carrots and onions and cook until vegetables are soft, 8 to 10 minutes. Season to taste with salt and pepper and set aside.

3. Drain potatoes then peel and return to the cleaned pot. Mash potatoes with a potato masher or a sturdy fork. Add the milk, remaining butter and cooked vegetables and mix until butter is completely melted and mixture is light and fluffy. Season to taste with salt and pepper. Serve alongside grilled sausages and red cabbage.

SEMOLINA PUDDING WITH RED CURRANT SAUCE

A "comfort food" dessert that's hearty but not too sweet.

Makes 5

1	cup red currant juice

One 1-inch-wide strip lemon peel

10	tbsp. sugar
4	tsp. potato flour
3	cups milk
1	vanilla pod, split lengthwise
5	tbsp. semolina flour
2	eggs, separated

Several sprigs fresh mint for garnish

1. Bring the red currant juice, lemon peel and 5 tbsp. sugar to a simmer over medium heat. Dissolve the potato flour in 2 tbsp. cold water in a small bowl. Slowly add the potato slurry to the red currant juice and cook, stirring constantly, until sauce thickens, about 2 minutes. Remove and discard the lemon peel. Spoon 2 tbsp. of the red currant sauce into each of five 8-ounce fluted ramekins and refrigerate until chilled.

2. Put the milk into a medium saucepan. Scrape the seeds from the vanilla pod with a small knife and add seeds and pod to the milk. Bring to just a boil over medium heat then stir in the semolina. Reduce heat to medium-low and cook, stirring constantly, until thick, about 5 minutes. Remove and discard vanilla pod then remove saucepan from the heat. Whisk the egg whites in bowl until soft peaks form. Beat the egg yolks and remaining sugar together in another bowl until thick. Fold the egg whites into the egg yolk mixture. Gradually add 1 cup of the semolina mixture to the eggs, then return entire mixture to the saucepan and stir until well mixed. Divide the pudding between the ramekins with the currant sauce, cover and refrigerate until firm, about 3 hours.

3. Invert the chilled puddings onto a plate and garnish each with a sprig of mint. Serve remaining currant sauce on the side.

HEVER CASTLE

Fairy tales and fanciful mazes under the castle walls

A CHILD'S BIRTHDAY PARTY IN A HEDGE MAZE

DINNER AT HEVER CASTLE

For a glimpse into England's past, there's no better place to visit than Hever Castle in Kent. Dating back to the 1270s, the castle is most famous for being the childhood home of Anne Boleyn, Henry VIII's unfortunate second wife, who grew up there in the early 1500s. Anne would no doubt be pleased to see how time has treated her family estate.

THE HEVER CASTLE LANDSCAPE

HEVER CASTLE RISES LIKE A MEMORY of centuries past above the wide moat that encircles it, towering over the surrounding Kentish landscape. Cross the drawbridge and you enter the castle grounds; pass under the iron teeth of the portcullis into the inner courtyard and suddenly the present day is swept out from under you.

But what truly sets Hever Castle apart are its extraordinary gardens, largely created between 1904 and 1908 by William Astor, son of multimillionaire John Jacob Astor and the castle's owner at the time. The great yew maze continues a tradition of English hedge mazes—take care you don't get lost in it—while the castle's topiary is trimmed to resemble sixteenth-century chess pieces. The Italian Garden, bordered by a 35-acre lake, serves as a backdrop for Astor's collection of Italian statuary, sarcophagi, columns and vases. The rock garden, planted with blue flowers between great slabs of rock, and the rose garden, with more than three thousand roses, add to the pageantry of color that defines this place.

In fact, the entire county of Kent is rife with gardens of all types and sizes, a testimony to the era when no great house (or noble castle) could possibly be considered complete without a cunningly designed and perfectly manicured garden. This land is truly a flower lover's paradise.

A CHILD'S BIRTHDAY PARTY IN A HEDGE MAZE

KENT IS A FAIRY-TALE PLACE, and for this child's birthday party I wanted each guest to feel as though she had stepped into a fairy tale. So to start with, we hid our birthday party setting in the center of the hedge maze at Hever Castle, with its manicured green hedges rising seven or eight feet high.

The table made of boxwoods seemed to spring right out of the earth. Satin pillows doubled as chargers at each place, and tiny parasols shielded the beautifully iced miniature cakes from the sun.

Of course, we got lost in the maze several times ourselves as we worked to create this table, running back and forth with our wheelbarrow full of candies, boxwoods, dishes and so on, until we knew the simple secret: turn right at every corner.

The meal for this tea party consisted of marshmallow sandwiches—the edge of the "bread" decorated with colorful nonpareils—and all the candy you could possibly eat. At each setting there was a cake iced with marzipan to look like a wrapped gift, almost too pretty to eat. And stacked here and there around the table were brightly wrapped gifts tied with gossamer ribbon.

Our tea set was decorated with fairies—exactly the kind you might see in a hedge maze like this, if they wished to be seen. Flower petal dishes formed each setting, atop a pillow charger. The centerpiece was made entirely of candy—lollipops, mints, chocolate almonds, marshmallows, an endless variety. The pink-and-white napkins were joined with a rose pin.

DINNER AT HEVER CASTLE

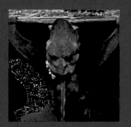

MOOD IS SUCH AN IMPORTANT but intangible thing at any dinner party, whether it's on the grounds of a castle or in your own dining room. For this dinner setting for two, I wanted to create something that lived partway between the romance of Romeo and Juliet and the legendary England of knights and castles.

Of course, having access to Hever Castle and its grounds helped—the mood is certainly set when you're dining in a rose garden under a castle's medieval walls—but at the same time, the table setting itself is at least as crucial, if not more so. This setting is a balancing act between feminine and masculine, between gentle and strong: on one side, the flowers everywhere, the lace and tapestry, the single white candle; on the other, the imposing antique chairs (borrowed from the castle's rooms), the heavy goblet-style wine glasses, the hunter-green candles at the two place settings. There's an understated tension to it all, a charge—just what a romantic dinner needs.

CREATING AN ENGLISH TABLE

FOR THIS ROMANTIC DINNER SETTING, I chose a tapestry tablecloth with a beautiful unicorn design. It lay atop a superb piece of antique lace done in pettipoint style, as light and airy as the angels embroidered throughout it.

The china was white, all the better to show off the abundant color of the flowers that were so much a part of this setting, both on the table and all around. A single square piece served as the charger; above that lay a round plate, then an oval, and finally a bowl fashioned to look like a flower's petals, which was filled with blossoms. (It's unusual to see a setting like this where all the pieces are of different shapes.) I'd had a sheet of handmade lace fashioned into napkins, and each was tied with a strand of ivy. The flatware was of a very traditional style, to merge thematically with the setting.

The wine glasses were clear crystal etched with an ivy design, and it is easy to imagine Hever Castle's early inhabitants drinking from the striking metal-framed goblets. The floral centerpiece had a single white candle rising out of its center; next to each setting, I placed a hunter-green candle set in an artichoke to add a little textural contrast.

A selection of gilt-edged, leather-bound, antiquarian books worked well to emphasize the days-gone-by feel of this dinner setting, as did the delicate lace underlay. The centerpiece was a mélange of pink and purple flowers from Hever Castle's gardens, the whole highlighted by gauzy Queen Anne's lace.

FOODS AND MARKETS OF KENT

KENT IS EVERYONE'S DREAM of agrarian England, a vision of rolling pastures and fertile hillsides, hop gardens, orchards, flower-strewn meadows and herds of sheep or cattle grazing on rich green grass.

Practically every town in Kent has its weekly market, and the larger ones—like Maidstone, Tonbridge and Sevenoaks—have been important market centers ever since the Middle Ages. But perhaps even more charming in these days of supermarkets and fast foods are the farmers' markets in the smaller villages of Kent. Every Thursday morning in Shipbourne (north of Tonbridge), for instance, local farmers set up stalls in the village church of St. Giles to sell their produce, meats, cheeses and herb breads. Other interesting Kentish markets include those in Royal Tunbridge Wells, held outside the town hall on the second Saturday of each month; in Wye, around the village green on the first and third Saturdays of the month; and in Bromley (actually a borough of Greater London), in the center of town every Friday and Saturday.

London

Bromley

Hever Castle   Sevenoaks   Maidstone

Tonbridge   Wye

Royal Tunbridge Wells

KENT

Of course, if you're visiting Kent, you'll undoubtedly be visiting London as well, and there's perhaps no city in the world more full of intriguing markets. Three of the most appealing are Bermondsey Market, which features antiques (with a tantalizing hint of disreputableness left over from the days when many of the goods here were stolen); Borough Market under the London Bridge railway station, with its gorgeous Victorian architecture and overflowing farmers' market on Saturdays; and Camden Market, with its wild, youthful vibe, where everything you can imagine and more is on sale every weekend.

London's legendary Harrods is a market unto itself. The candies and sweets for our Hever Castle child's birthday party were all sourced there. Founded in 1849, Harrods still reflects its origins as a food emporium, offering 150 different kinds of tea, 300 cheeses, more than 1,500 different wines, an amazing array of chocolates and candies — a truly stunning abundance.

RECIPES

MINIATURE SCONES

CHILLED ASPARAGUS SOUP

POACHED SALMON WITH
DILL VINAIGRETTE

SALT-ROASTED POTATOES

RIB ROAST WITH
YORKSHIRE PUDDING

TRIFLE

MINIATURE SCONES

*Clotted cream, also known as Devon cream, is a specialty
of Devonshire, England, and is made by heating unpasteurized
cream and skimming the fat that rises to the surface.*

Makes about 2 dozen

16	tbsp. (2 sticks) butter
3	cups flour
10	tbsp. sugar
2½	tsp. baking powder
½	tsp. baking soda
½	tsp. salt
1	cup buttermilk
1	tsp. finely grated lemon zest
	Best-quality fruit jam or jelly
1	cup clotted cream

1. Preheat oven to 425° F. Melt 4 tbsp. of the butter in a small saucepan and set aside. Cut remaining butter into small pieces, transfer to a small plate and chill in the freezer.

2. Sift the flour, 6 tbsp. of the sugar, baking powder, baking soda and salt together into a large bowl. Using your fingers, work chilled butter into the flour mixture until it resembles coarse cornmeal. Add the buttermilk and lemon zest and stir with a fork until a crumbly dough forms. Do not overwork the dough or else the scones will be tough.

3. Turn the dough out onto a floured work surface. Roll out to ½-inch thickness. Cut out scones using a variety of 1½- to 2-inch cookie cutters such as triangles, diamonds, rounds and hearts. Brush the tops of each scone with some of the melted butter and sprinkle on some of the remaining sugar. Transfer scones to a baking sheet and bake until golden brown around the edges, 12 to 15 minutes. Serve warm with jelly or jam and clotted cream.

CHILLED ASPARAGUS SOUP

*To find the right place to trim the ends of asparagus, hold
the stalk at the end and a few inches up. Bend it; it will break
at the right point.*

Serves 6

2	pounds asparagus, woody ends trimmed
1	tbsp. butter
1	medium yellow onion, peeled and chopped
4	cups chicken stock
	Salt and freshly ground white pepper
½	cup heavy cream
6	thin strips of lemon zest

1. Cut the tips from the asparagus and set aside. Coarsely chop the stalks and set aside separately. Melt the butter in a small pot over medium heat. Add the onions and asparagus stalks and cook for 1 minute. Cover the pan and steam until onions are soft, about 5 minutes. Add the stock, season to taste with salt and pepper and simmer until vegetables are very soft, 15 to 20 minutes. Working in batches, puree the soup in a blender. As each batch is pureed, pass through a fine sieve into a clean bowl. Stir in the cream and adjust the seasoning. Cover and refrigerate until chilled, 1 to 2 hours.

2. Bring a small pot of water to a boil. Add asparagus tips and cook until bright green and just cooked through, about 1 minute. Drain and plunge them into a bowl of ice water to stop them from cooking. Drain again. Garnish each serving with some of the tips and lemon zest.

POACHED SALMON WITH DILL VINAIGRETTE

This is a dish that can be served hot or cold; to serve it cold, simply wrap the salmon in plastic wrap after removing it from the poaching liquid and refrigerate for up to a day before serving.

Serves 4

1½	cups white wine
1	carrot, peeled and sliced
1	onion, peeled and sliced
1	rib celery, sliced
3	sprigs parsley
1	bay leaf
1	tsp. black peppercorns
Salt	
1¼	pound fresh salmon filet
1	tbsp. minced fresh dill
½	tsp. dried mustard
4	tsp. white wine vinegar
2	tbsp. olive oil
Freshly ground black pepper	
2	cups mixed greens

1. Boil the wine, 3 cups water, carrots, onions, celery, parsley, bay leaf, peppercorns and ½ tsp. salt together in a medium-wide pot over medium-high heat for 10 minutes. Remove the pot from the heat and set poaching liquid aside to let cool for 20 minutes.

2. Add the salmon to the poaching liquid and bring to just a simmer over medium heat. Cover pot, reduce heat to low and gently poach 15 minutes for medium-rare, 20 minutes for medium.

3. Meanwhile, whisk the dill, mustard and vinegar together in a small bowl. Slowly add the oil, whisking constantly, until emulsified. Season the vinaigrette to taste with salt and pepper and set aside.

4. Lift the salmon from the poaching liquid, discarding the liquid, and flake into four equal-sized pieces. Arrange a bed of greens on each of four salad plates. Arrange a piece of salmon over greens and drizzle some of the dressing over each.

SALT-ROASTED POTATOES

The English coastal town of Maldon, Essex, has been a leading salt producer since the Middle Ages. The distinctive pyramid-shaped crystals of Maldon sea salt have the delicate flavor of sea spray.

Serves 6

3	pounds small new potatoes

Kosher salt

4	tbsp. butter, melted
2	tbsp. coarse sea salt, such as Maldon sea salt or *fleur de sel*

Freshly ground black pepper

2	tsp. chopped fresh chives

I. Preheat oven to 425° F. Put the potatoes into a large pot and add cold water to cover by 2 inches. Generously season with kosher salt and bring to a boil over medium-high heat. Cook until potatoes are just cooked through, about 20 minutes. Drain and transfer to a medium baking dish.

2. Pour the butter over the potatoes and roll them around until well coated. Add the sea salt, season to taste with pepper and toss again. Bake until potatoes begin to turn golden brown, 20 to 25 minutes. Garnish with the chives.

RIB ROAST WITH YORKSHIRE PUDDING

The key to fluffy Yorkshire pudding is a very hot pan and very hot fat drippings. If your pan has cooled down, heat the pan and grease in the oven for ten minutes before adding the batter.

Serves 6

7	pound rib roast, left out at room temperature for 2 hours

Salt and freshly ground black pepper

1	cup flour
2	eggs
1¼	cups milk

I. Preheat oven to 325° F. Heat a heavy medium-size baking pan over high heat for 5 minutes. Generously season the roast with salt and pepper. Sear the meat on all sides in the hot pan until well browned all over. Turn the meat, fat side up, ribs down, and transfer to the oven. Roast until instant-read thermometer registers 125° F for medium-rare, about I hour and 45 minutes.

2. Meanwhile, prepare the Yorkshire pudding. Put the flour, eggs, milk, ½ tsp. salt and I tbsp. water into the jar of a blender and process until batter is completely smooth.

3. Working quickly, transfer the roast to a carving board, loosely cover with foil and set aside to let rest 30 minutes before carving. Move the oven rack to the upper third of the oven and increase the oven temperature to 400° F. Pour the batter into the still very hot pan and fat drippings. Bake the pudding until puffy, crispy and deep golden brown on top. Cut the Yorkshire pudding into equal squares and serve immediately alongside the carved roast.

TRIFLE

Trifle is a classic English dessert, whose modern version dates back to the middle of the eighteenth century. Variations of the trifle, which is always made with some amount of liquor, were dubbed "tipsy hedgehog" or "tipsy parson"—the latter evidently for the effect it may have had on visiting men of the cloth.

Serves 6

1	cup blueberries
1	cup raspberries
1½	cups strawberries, hulled and sliced
6	tbsp. sugar
1½	cups milk
2	cups heavy cream
4	egg yolks
2	tsp. cornstarch
1	loaf pound cake, sliced into ½-inch-thick slices
8	tbsp. sweet sherry

1. Toss the berries and 3 tbsp. of the sugar together in a bowl and set aside to macerate for at least 1 hour. Bring the milk and 1 cup of the cream to just a boil in a medium saucepan over medium-high heat. Meanwhile, whisk the egg yolks, cornstarch and remaining sugar together in a medium bowl until thick and pale yellow. Slowly add 1 cup of the hot milk mixture to the eggs, whisking constantly, then return entire mixture to the saucepan. Reduce heat to low and cook, stirring constantly, until custard is thick enough to coat the back of a wooden spoon, 8 to 10 minutes. Transfer the custard to a bowl, cover the surface with plastic wrap to prevent a skin from forming and refrigerate until cool.

2. Whisk remaining heavy cream in a medium bowl until stiff peaks form, and then set aside. Line the bottom of a medium trifle bowl with a single layer of cake. Drizzle one quarter of the sherry over the cake, and then spread one quarter of the berries evenly over cake. Spoon one quarter of the custard over the berries and cover the custard with one quarter of the whipped cream. Repeat the layers three more times, topping the trifle with dollops of whipped cream. Cover and refrigerate for at least 3 hours before serving. This allows the cake to absorb all of the flavors.

SALZBURG

*A musical mood
in flower-strewn hills
and under castle walls*

PICNIC
IN THE
SALZBURG
HILLS

DINNER NEAR
LEOPOLDSKRON
PALACE

Salzburg is a strain of Mozart's flute concerto overheard as you walk down an airy city street; or perhaps it's recalling that certain scene in "The Sound of Music" as you look up at the walls of the Leopoldskron Palace. Salzburg exists so much in art it almost seems to be an artwork itself, yet it's a real city, vibrant, thriving and bursting with life.

THE SALZBURG LANDSCAPE

SALZBURG WAS NAMED FOR SALT (*salz*, in German), that crucial condiment, mined out of the nearby mountains, on which the city's early fortunes were founded. It lies tucked beneath the rocky crag of the Mönchsberg, atop which sits the imposing Hohensalzburg fortress. Yet despite this looming military overseer, the city maintains an air of lightness and charm. Baroque buildings line the streets of the old town, gentle footbridges arch over the Salzach River, cafés serve dark coffee and sweet strudels and tortes, and the delicate gold-and-wrought-iron signs that decorate the Getreiderstrasse make it seem almost as if you'd stepped into a movie—as well you might have, since many of the most famous scenes in *The Sound of Music* were filmed here.

This small city's connection to music, however, goes back much farther than that. In 1756, Wolfgang Amadeus Mozart was born here, and his memory and music permeate the character of this place at all times—not just during the yearly Salzburg Festival, one of Europe's most famous musical events. But as the heroine of *The Sound of Music* famously noted, the most compelling music to be heard here is found outside Salzburg, in the rolling hills that surround the city. It's not instrumental music, bur rather the sound of the soft breeze through the wildflowers as you sit and enjoy a picnic by a lake, with the blue Alps rising serenely in the background.

PICNIC IN THE SALZBURG HILLS

BEING IN AUSTRIA inevitably made me think of my favorite scenes in *The Sound of Music*—and what could be more glorious than a picnic in the actual hillside meadow where Julie Andrews once sang of the hills being alive with the sound of music?

I covered the table with a handmade creamy-white lace tablecloth, allowing it to flow right down to the green grass and wildflowers. Then, to continue the theme of the table merging with the meadow, I chose green glass dishes with a crisscross pattern for each setting and silverware with a green and white pattern. The effect was almost that of a gazebo rising up from the meadow.

The cut-glass plates had the same pattern as the flower-filled centerpiece and the cake stand laden with assorted Austrian pastries. With the morning light shining over everything, it was perfect. The only thing missing was the music, but we could imagine that.

Part of the fun of this table setting involved using the cake stand, glass vase of flowers and centerpiece basket to create a design on several levels, or tiers. In a way, this subtly evokes the many-layered tortes for which Austria is so famous. The green crisscross pattern on the silverware also continues the design of the plates and glasses.

DINNER NEAR LEOPOLDSKRON PALACE

NOTHING SUGGESTS THE GLORIES and complexities of Austria's past more than Schloss Leopoldskron. I couldn't think of a more appropriate place to create a dinner setting for eight that would tie together the history of Salzburg, the theme of music and musical instruments, and the colors of cream and gold so prevalent throughout the palace. Another appealing connection was the fact that part of *The Sound of Music* was filmed in the magnificent gardens of Leopoldskron.

The palace staff was nice enough to let us borrow tables and chairs for our dinner, and they were perfect in the way they captured, along with the setting itself, the Baroque splendor of eighteenth-century Salzburg. The effect I was aiming for was that combination of elegance and playfulness that seemed to define life in the Austria of that era—the sense that you could put together a sumptuous dinner like this one with the ease and effortlessness with which Mozart, Salzburg's favorite son, seemed to toss off one masterpiece after another.

CREATING A SALZBURG TABLE

AS MUSIC WAS ONE of the central themes of this setting, I used old sheets of classical music as underlays for the gold chargers and black-and-white plates. The design on the plates also suggests musical notes, and the creamy color of the antique paper plays off the cream-and-gold-colored candles.

The tablecloth was a burgundy-and-gold brocade fabric, while the napkins were burgundy taffeta with gold cherubs in the design. My vision of the colors for this table was of black and white, gold and burgundy, and almost every element plays into that theme.

We were generously allowed to borrow the silver centerpiece candelabra from one of the rooms in the palace, balancing it with the silver antique violin in the center of the table. The glassware, with its design that suggests the f-shaped holes in a violin, was purchased at a little shop in Salzburg, as were the golden cherub statuettes and the small decorative glass balls (which are actually Christmas ornaments).

The dark flowers are chocolate cosmos, which really do smell of chocolate. The flower vendor hadn't seen them in over twenty years, he said—so we bought every bloom he had.

The miniature musical instruments atop
the napkins at each place were bought
at a Christmas shop in Salzburg—itself
a year-round miniature of the city's
famous Christmas market. The black-
handled flatware continued the lyrical
theme of the plates and sheet music—
even the design at the end of the handle
seems to suggest a musical staff.

FOODS AND MARKETS OF SALZBURG

AS DECORATIVE AS SALZBURG may seem, it is very much a lively market town—it has been so since at least as far back as the year 996, when the Holy Roman Emperor Otto III granted Salzburg the right to hold a market. And although you might not think it, Austria has an impressive culinary tradition, influenced by the many nations that were once part of the vast, polyglot Austro-Hungarian Empire. There are also many regional variations within this small country—for instance, you'll rarely find *Steirisches verhackert* (Styrian diced ham with minced garlic and pumpkin seed oil) around Salzburg, but if you head over to the neighboring state of Styria, it's on almost every menu.

What you will find in Salzburg, however, is food that is varied and intriguing. Soup with semolina or liver dumplings is very popular, as is *knoblauchsuppe*, or garlic soup; the seasonal *bärlauchsuppe*, or wild garlic soup, is a delicious variation. Veal goulash; pork roast with dumplings and white cabbage; roast goose with red cabbage and dumplings; beef liver with onions, capers, lemon juice, white wine and polenta (Italy is also an important influence here)—these are all examples of traditional Salzburg main courses, and all, it should be noted, are quite substantial.

And then there are the desserts, for which Austria is justly renowned. In Salzburg the most famous dessert of them all is *Salzburger nockerln*, a delectably creamy soufflé sprinkled with confectioners' sugar—one of those deceptive sweets that seem as light as air but are very rich indeed.

CHRISTMAS MARKET

This market dates back to before 1500, and while it's existed in several locations, currently you'll find it on the Cathedral and Residenz Squares each year from the end of November until Christmas Eve. Wooden toys, glassware, ceramics and decorative items of all kinds—including, of course, Christmas ornaments—are all sold here. Bundle up against the icy cold and enjoy a cup of hot, spiced wine as your boots crunch through the snow among the green wooden stalls.

GREEN MARKET

Held every day except Sundays in front of the Collegiate Church, this is where you'll find fresh fruits and vegetables, meats, poultry, fish (mostly freshwater, from nearby mountain streams), cheese and pretty much every other kind of foodstuff. If you get hungry as you browse, look for the sausage vendors selling delicious hot sausages from carts. There's also an organic farmers' market every Friday morning on Papageno Square, as well as several other satellite markets throughout the city.

THE "SCHRANNE"

This colorful market takes place in the square in front of the Mirabell Palace every Thursday morning, with farmers from throughout the surrounding region arriving to sell their wares. It's a bustling scene. Particularly worth noting are some of the baked goods, like apple-flavored pretzels, iced gingerbread hearts (lebkuchen) and bauernkrapfen, which are the local deep-fried doughnuts, round in shape with an indentation in the middle rather than a hole, sometimes filled with jam.

SALZBURG

Mirabell Palace

Kapuzinerberg

Marktsteg

Mozart's Birthplace

Getreidegasse

Salzach Mozartsteg

River

Collegiate Church

Residenz

Cathedral

Mönchsberg

Leopoldskron Palace

Hohensalzburg

WINES
OF AUSTRIA

Austria is one of the great wine-producing countries of the world, though for many years its wines were barely known in the United States and still remain somewhat obscure. But if you like crisp, aromatic white wines, there's no better place to investigate.

GRÜNER VELTLINER

Grüner veltliner is a sexy grape with a decidedly unsexy name—so much so that some U.S. importers have suggested simply shortening it to "GrüVe." Its unwieldy name notwithstanding, grüner veltliner is Austria's most widely planted grape, and it produces some wonderful white wines: full of fruit, but with a backbone of spice and mineral, and capable of aging in a cellar for years. Some of the best "GrüVe" producers are Hirtzberger, Knoll, Prager, F.X. Pichler, Bründlmayer, Schloss Gobelsburg and Nigl.

SAUVIGNON BLANC

Austrian sauvignon blanc leans away from the in-your-face gooseberry–green pepper flavors common to New World sauvignons from New Zealand, say; instead it's concentrated and elegant, with an edge that can recall the light citrus bitterness of grapefruit rind. The best come from Styria, and producers to look for include Tement, Polz and Sattlerhof.

RIESLING

Austria, Germany and France's Alsace are the three great riesling-producing regions of the world; each has its own style, its own superb vineyards and brilliant winemakers. Austrian rieslings tends to be less sweet than German versions, with floral aromas and green apple and mineral flavors that are honed to a point by sharp, mouthwatering acidity. The producers listed for grüner veltliner all make great rieslings as well.

RED WINES

Austria also produces red wines, although they are even less well known in the United States than the whites. The best Austrian reds come from two unusual grape varieties: zweigelt and blaufränkisch. Zweigelt tends to produce medium-bodied, lightly spicy wines; blaufränkisch makes darker, denser wines with scents of cassis and black pepper, and dark berry flavors.

LOIBNER
GRÜNER VELTLINER 0,75l

WEINGUT KNOLL
A-3601 UNTER-LOIBEN · WACHAU

RECIPES

HORSERADISH DEVILED EGGS

Austrian cuisine features many dishes flavored with horseradish, like this variation on deviled eggs.

Serves 4

8	eggs, hard-boiled, peeled and halved lengthwise
6	tbsp. mayonnaise
4 to 6 tbsp. freshly grated horseradish
Salt and freshly ground white pepper
4	chives, thinly sliced

Put the egg yolks into a bowl and mash with a fork. Add the mayonnaise and horseradish, season to taste with salt and pepper and whisk until smooth. Fill each egg white half with some of the egg yolk mixture. Garnish with the chives. Serve chilled.

SAUSAGE SALAD

The sausage vendor's cart is a highlight of every open-air market in Salzburg. Here's a lighter approach to the Salzburger sausage vendor's wares.

Serves 4

6	new potatoes
8	ounces smoked German-style sausage or kielbasa
½	pound green beans, trimmed and halved crosswise
2	tomatoes, cored and cut into wedges
2	tbsp. red wine vinegar
4	tbsp. vegetable oil
Salt and freshly ground black pepper

1. Put the potatoes into a small pot, cover with water and bring to a boil over high heat. Boil until cooked through, about 25 minutes. Meanwhile, cook the sausages in another pot of boiling water until heated through, 6 to 8 minutes. Transfer to a cutting board. Add the green beans to the boiling water and cook until tender, 3 to 4 minutes. Drain and transfer to a bowl. Drain the potatoes, peel and slice and add to bowl with green beans. Slice the sausage and add to bowl with potatoes. Add the tomatoes.

2. Whisk the vinegar and oil together in a small bowl. Season to taste with salt and pepper and pour the dressing over the vegetables and sausages. Toss until well coated and set aside to let marinate for 2 hours before serving.

SALZBURG GARLIC SOUP WITH PUMPERNICKEL MEATBALLS

This is one of the traditional dishes of Salzburg, featured on practically every restaurant menu.

Serves 6

4	tbsp. butter
1	medium yellow onion, peeled and chopped
1	head garlic, cloves separated, peeled and coarsely chopped
1¼	cups flour
½	cup white wine
4	cups beef broth
½	pound ground beef
½	cup fresh pumpernickel breadcrumbs

Pinch dried marjoram

1	egg, beaten

Salt and freshly ground black pepper

3	tbsp. vegetable oil
½	cup sour cream
1	pinch grated nutmeg
¼	bunch fresh chives, chopped

1. Melt the butter in a medium pot over medium heat. Add the onions and garlic and cook until lightly golden, about 10 minutes. Add ¼ cup of flour and cook, stirring constantly, until flour is lightly toasted, about 5 minutes. Whisk in the white wine and cook for 1 minute. Slowly add the broth, whisking constantly to prevent any lumps from forming, and bring to a simmer. Cook until soup thickens and reduces by 25 percent, about 30 minutes.

2. Meanwhile, put the beef, breadcrumbs, marjoram, egg, ½ tsp. salt and ⅛ tsp. pepper into a bowl and mix with a fork until just combined. Divide and shape the meat mixture into 18 meatballs, each about an inch in diameter. Dredge each meatball in the remaining flour and set aside. Heat the oil in a medium skillet over medium-high heat. Add the meatballs and cook, swirling the skillet over the heat, until meatballs are browned all over, about 5 minutes. Reduce heat to medium-low, cover skillet and cook until fully cooked through, about 5 minutes more. Transfer meatballs to a small plate, loosely cover with foil to keep warm and set aside.

3. Puree the soup in a blender and return to the pot. Stir in the sour cream and nutmeg and season to taste with salt and pepper. Heat over medium-high heat and bring to just a boil. Divide the soup among six soup bowls. Put three meatballs into each bowl, garnish with some of the chopped chives and serve immediately.

CUCUMBER SALAD

This is a cool and appealingly crisp salad. Make sure, though, to use English (or hothouse) cucumbers, as the standard kind has too much water and too many seeds.

Serves 4

1	English cucumber, trimmed and halved crosswise

Salt

2	tbsp. white wine vinegar
1	tsp. spicy German mustard
¼	tsp. sugar

Freshly ground black pepper

2	tbsp. vegetable oil
½	small yellow onion, peeled and thinly sliced

1. Using a vegetable peeler, shave the cucumber lengthwise into thin, wide strips. Transfer the cucumber strips to a colander, sprinkle on 1 tsp. salt and set aside until the strips give off some of their water and become pliable, about 15 minutes.

2. Meanwhile, whisk the vinegar, mustard, sugar, and salt and pepper to taste together in a bowl. Add the oil in a slow steady stream and whisk until emulsified. Add the onions to the vinaigrette and set aside. Squeeze out the excess water from the cucumbers and add to the bowl with the onions. Toss and let marinate in the refrigerator for 1 hour before serving.

WIENER SCHNITZEL

You may also find this dish garnished with a fried egg, anchovies and capers (Holstein), or topped with sautéed peppers and onions (puszta) or smothered in a mushroom cream sauce (jaeger).

Serves 4

8	tbsp. butter
1	cup flour

Salt and freshly ground black pepper

2	eggs
3	cups fresh breadcrumbs

Four 4-ounce pieces of veal top round, pounded to ¼-inch thickness

10	tbsp. vegetable oil
2	lemons, halved
1	cup whole-berry cranberry sauce

1. Melt the butter in a small saucepan over medium heat. Skim foam that rises to the surface and cook until foam subsides. Carefully pour melted butter into a small bowl, leaving milky solids behind. Set the clarified butter aside.

2. Put the flour into a dish, season to taste with salt and pepper and set aside. Beat the eggs in a second dish and set aside. Put the breadcrumbs into a third dish, season to taste with salt and pepper and set aside. Season the veal with salt and pepper. Dredge 1 piece of veal at a time in flour, shaking off excess, then dip into egg, evenly coating each side, then coat with the breadcrumbs.

3. Working with two skillets at a time, heat half of the oil and half of the clarified butter in each skillet over medium-high heat. Place two pieces of veal in each skillet and cook, shaking skillet over heat, until golden brown, about 1½ minutes per side. Serve immediately with the lemon wedges and cranberry sauce on the side.

SALZBURGER NOCKERLN
(SALZBURG SOUFFLÉ)

According to the 1938 operetta A Season in Salzburg, *this delightful dessert soufflé is "as sweet as love and as tender as a kiss"—and it is so true.*

Serves 4

1	tsp. butter
2	tbsp. red currant or grape jelly
4	egg whites, at room temperature
7	tbsp. granulated sugar
2	egg yolks
3	tbsp. flour
½	tsp. vanilla extract
½	tsp. freshly grated lemon zest
1	tbsp. confectioners' sugar

1. Preheat the oven to 400° F. Grease a 5-cup casserole dish with the butter. Evenly spread the jelly over the bottom of the dish and set aside.

2. Beat the egg whites in a bowl with an electric mixer on high speed until medium-stiff peaks form. Add 4 tbsp. of the granulated sugar and continue beating until stiff peaks form. Whisk the yolks, flour, vanilla extract, lemon zest and remaining granulated sugar together in another bowl until well combined and thick. Fold the egg yolk mixture into the egg white mixture with a rubber spatula until just combined. Pour the batter into the prepared dish and bake until puffed and golden brown, about 12 minutes. Dust with the confectioners' sugar and serve immediately.

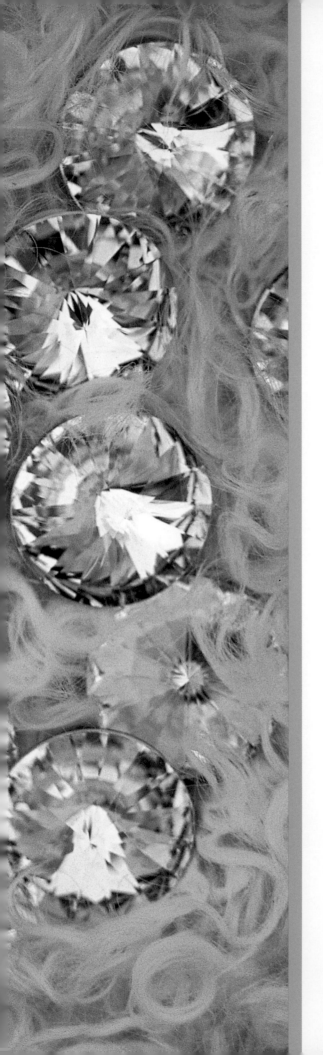

ST. MORITZ

Glamour and glitz,
champagne and diamonds
in a snowy paradise

CHAMPAGNE
BRUNCH
FOR TWELVE

"MARRY ME"
DINNER
FOR TWO

Descending by train into the Engadine Valley feels like descending into some hidden kingdom, the bejeweled capital of which is St. Moritz. Nestled by a lake, under the mountain walls, the town's streets speak the language of international glamour and glitz. Can you find a diamond in the snow? If you've found St. Moritz, it's proof you can.

THE ST. MORITZ LANDSCAPE

ST. MORITZ in winter is the black of pine forests set against the pristine white snow slopes of the Upper Engadine Valley in the Swiss canton of Graubünden, sandwiched between Austria and Italy. The air is dazzlingly clear in St. Moritz—the town lies more than three thousand feet above sea level—and the sun shines brightly (more than three hundred and thirty days each year) on both the beautiful landscape and the beautiful rich and famous people who flock to this classic jet-set resort town.

St. Moritz is all about contrast. The surrounding mountains and forests are nature at her most stark and beautiful. The town itself, however, is a different story. While traces of the small Swiss village it once was still exist here and there, St. Moritz has been a deluxe destination for international travelers for several centuries now. The shops that line its streets wouldn't seem out of place on Fifth Avenue in New York or the rue du Faubourg Saint-Honoré in Paris. Names like Prada, Harry Winston, Armani and others draw the attention of passers-by who seem to be in a constant competition over whose skiwear is the most chic, whose fur the most splendid. And the nightlife, of course, lasts until the first rays of dawn. Yet, somehow, the marriage of St. Moritz's glitter and flash with the majestic austerity of its Swiss mountain setting does seem to work. Opposites attract, as they say.

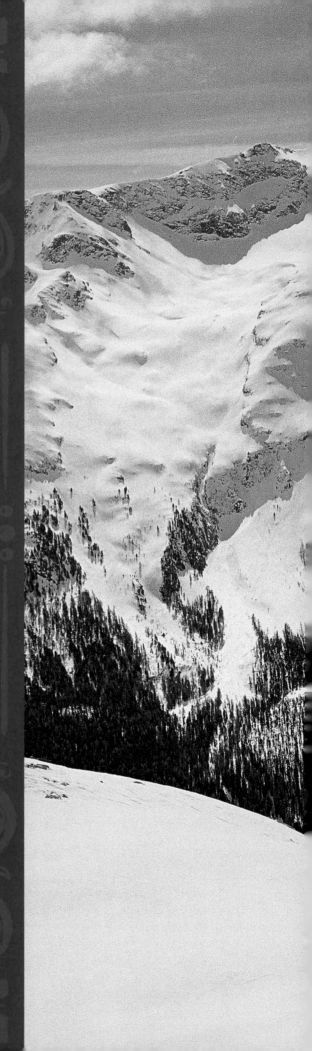

CHAMPAGNE BRUNCH FOR TWELVE

IF YOU'RE IN A TOWN known for its champagne climate, what better event to throw than a champagne brunch? The extraordinary Badrutt's Palace hotel served as the backdrop for this extravagant table setting, and the hotel staff had the kindness to lend me silverware from their vault, as well as the grand table and chairs.

The huge cashmere-sheepskin throw covering the table did double duty: recalling the snowy landscape all around and conveying the feel of luxury a champagne brunch deserves. Antique champagne buckets served as vases for the flowers—although, of course, a few were also used for the champagne!

For the brunch itself, we served an appropriately luxurious bill of fare: chilled lobster, caviar with all its accompaniments, champagne (what else?), and, as is traditional in St. Moritz, icy cold vodka served in slender wine glasses.

Silver and white are the colors of winter, but even with a limited palette, there is still a world of options. Here I used white roses, gerber daisies and casablanca lilies. Each place setting features a silver egg cup with an empty eggshell serving as a tiny flower vase. Piles of bright Swarovski crystals adorn each place setting, but any colorful crystal could be used for the same effect.

"MARRY ME" DINNER FOR TWO

CONTRAST HELPS FIX EVENTS in our minds, and if anything is supposed to linger in memory, it's the moment a couple decides to get married. So, with this in mind, why not contrast the heat of romance with the chilly splendor of St. Moritz's snowfields and ski runs? Besides, it's not for nothing that jewel thieves refer to diamonds as ice.

For this proposal dinner set in a snowfield between Badrutt's Palace hotel and the winter-frozen lake that borders St. Moritz, I thought in terms of black and white, stark and elegant. Two antique white vases full of ranaculus, white veronica, viburnam, lisianthus and white roses balance two beautiful white candle arrangements— after all, any marriage survives and thrives on a balance between the two partners. An antique champagne bucket with a cold bottle stands at the ready, as a celebration will soon be in order.

CREATING A
ST. MORITZ TABLE

FOR THIS TABLE SETTING, the intriguing chairs with their woven design—appropriate for two people planning to join in matrimony—were borrowed from Badrutt's Palace, as was the table itself. The table topper was a cashmere shawl in a black and white design, with a piece of black and white French toile de Jouy fabric underneath it. My aim was to combine the romanticism of the printed toile de Jouy with the sensual texture of the cashmere.

Each place features a silver charger and two white plates, black-handled silverware and an individual flower arrangement in a silver and crystal cocktail cup. The napkin rings are crystal faux-diamonds, recalling the real diamonds of an engagement ring, of course. The lampshades for the candles are made of the same black and white toile de Jouy fabric that underlies the cashmere, with chandelier crystals (easy to find at any lamp store) added on as decoration.

The etched crystal glassware enhances the romantic mood of the setting, as does the snow scattered here and there on the table. And finally, the *pièce de résistance:* an engagement ring of diamonds and a single sapphire, nestled in snow in a silver-domed glass cup.

White candles blend perfectly with the pure white snow all around, but white roses are just ivory enough to stand out. Around the table are other flower arrangements in silvery candle holders shining bright against the light-reflecting snow. The furrier in town was happy to send over a selection of lushly luxurious furs to choose from.

FOODS OF
ST. MORITZ

SWISS CUISINE IS MORE than just cheese and chocolate—though the Swiss are rightly famous for those two products. Influenced by Italy to the south, France to the west, and Germany and Austria to the north and east, Swiss cuisine is a mélange of different flavors and styles, although the more traditional dishes are firmly rooted in the country's rural Alpine heritage. Switzerland, of course, is one of the world's major cheese makers, producing hundreds of cheeses of varying types (most, however, are made of cow's milk). Not surprisingly, dairy products play a role in most Swiss dishes. And while Swiss cuisine is very regional—you won't necessarily find the same dishes in Basel as you would in Geneva or in Ticino—St. Moritz is so cosmopolitan that you'll find foods here from every corner of the country, not to mention the rest of the world.

CHEESE

The classic Swiss cheeses include gruyère, *one of the world's great cooking cheeses (and essential for fondue), with a fruity, sharp taste;* vacherin mont-d'or, *a soft, mild and very creamy cheese;* tête de moine *("monk's head"), a highly aromatic cheese usually shaved off in curls with a tool called a girolle;* emmentaler, *what the world thinks of as "Swiss" cheese, i.e., the one with the holes;* raclette, *a semisoft cheese typically served melted on top of boiled potatoes (the dish is also called "raclette");* tilsiter *or* royalp, *a mild cheese with small holes;* sbrinz, *a spicy, tangy cheese used mostly for grating; and* appenzeller, *a strongly fruity cheese whose rind is washed in cider or wine as it ages. In addition to fondue and raclette, other Swiss cheese-based dishes include* croûte au fromage *or* käseschnitten *(cheese melted on toast),* chäs-chüechli *(cheese tartlets) and* malakoffs *(cheese fritters).*

MEATS

Sausages such as kalberwurst, chüblig, mettwurst, bratwurst, wienerli, emmentalerli *and* landjaeger *often appear in* wurstsalat, *a sausage salad with potatoes, onions and cheese.* Bundnerfleisch *is air-dried, thinly sliced beef, similar to Italy's bresaola. Traditional dishes include* zürigschnätzlets *(veal in cream and white wine);* escalope augonoise *(veal with ham, tomatoes and raclette cheese); and* rippli *(smoked pork with bacon, beans and potatoes).*

CHOCOLATE

Since the first chocolate shop opened in the Swiss capital of Bern in 1792, Switzerland has become one of the world's leading chocolate producers—if not in volume, then at least in quality. The Swiss are also the world's leading consumers of chocolate, eating more of it per person than any other nation on the planet. And over eighty percent of that is smooth, rich, sweet milk chocolate. It's used in desserts, of course (chocolate fondue is a classic), but most of it by far is sold in bars for nibbling, with Toblerone, Lindt *and* Nestlé *among the most famous brands.*

DESSERTS

Aside from chocolate fondue, there are many other delicious Swiss desserts. Nusstorte *is a walnut tart local to the region around St. Moritz. The deep-fried, fritterlike apple cookies called* apfelküchlein *are found throughout the country and are wonderful either hot or cold.* Basler leckerli *are a delicious flat cookie from Basel flavored with almonds, candied citrus peels, cinnamon, cloves and lots of honey. Carrot cake is actually very Swiss (and very good)— here it's known as* rüebli kuchen. *And don't miss* rathhaustorte, *a hazelnut cake filled with hazelnut meringue and covered in a chocolate glaze.*

SHOPS OF ST. MORITZ

UNLIKE THE OTHER TOWNS in this book, St. Moritz isn't known for its open-air markets or its wonderful local produce. But that doesn't mean it doesn't offer superb shopping. Most of the best shops are concentrated on the via Maistra, walking distance from all of the major hotels, including Badrutt's Palace.

A few of the premier shopping venues include Harry Winston, for jewelry; Prada, Versace, Jill Sander, Gucci, Valentino, Hermès, Bottega Veneta and Pucci for designer clothing; a plethora of boutiques for Swiss watches, Cuban cigars, fine wines, caviar—the list could go on for pages. It's window-shopping at its finest (or real shopping, for those who can afford it). And, of course, watching the people doing the window-shopping, dressed to the nines in furs and designer skiwear, is almost more fun than the shopping itself.

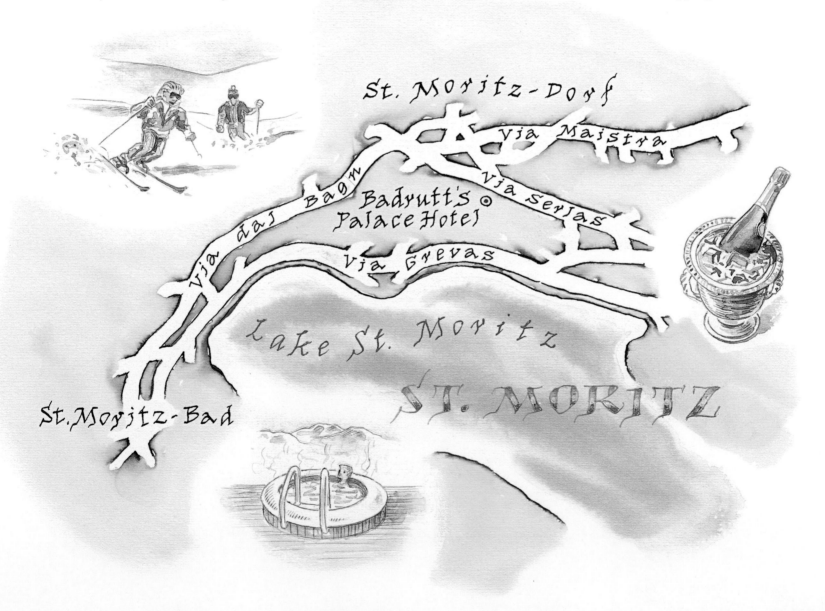

WINES OF SWITZERLAND

SWISS WINES ARE LITTLE KNOWN in the United States, but that has more to do with the exchange rate than the quality of the wine itself—at their best, Swiss wines, particularly whites, are quite competitive with the wines from anywhere else in Europe. Interestingly, Switzerland is also home to the longest-running wine festival anywhere, the Fête des Vignerons, which has been held in the town of Vevey every twenty-five years since 1797. To attend the next Fête, however, you'll have to be patient, as it won't take place until 2024.

The Valais, as the valley of the Rhône River is known in Switzerland, produces most of Switzerland's best wines, along with La Vaux, above the shores of Lake Geneva. Both regions are in the southwest of the country, and have steep rocky slopes and terraced vineyards climbing into the Alpine sky. The primary grape planted in both the Valais and La Vaux is chasselas. Otherwise known as fendant, this grape accounts for almost forty-five percent of the white wine production in the Valais, and, in good hands, produces wines that are light and fruity, sometimes ending on an almondy note. Interesting whites are also produced from petite arvine, which is usually richer, with a lime-and-mineral character. A few of the best producers are Badoux, Bovard and Gilliard.

For Swiss reds, the region to look to is Ticino, on the Italian border. It's a much sunnier, warmer region with more rainfall than the Valais and a lot of Italian influence (the local language is Italian). The majority of the grapes planted here are merlot, and have been since the late nineteenth century. The merlots of Ticino are round and mouthfilling, full of ripe cherry flavor. Some names to look for include Brivio, Zanini and Tamobrini.

These three wines are all made from the same grape: chasselas. One is a fendant from the Valais region (where chasselas is called fendant); the others are named for their regions: Aigle, a part of the Vaud, on the shores of Lake Geneva, and Neuchâtel, on the shores of the lake of the same name. No matter where it's grown, though, when it's made well, chasselas produces a light, straw-colored wine that is crisp and refreshing, like a breath of Alpine air.

Château d'Auverni

Aigle les M...

APPELLATION D'ORIGINE CONT...

GRAND VIN

PRODUCT OF SWITZERLAND

SWISS WHITE WINE

F.Rouge

Imported by

SOLE AGENTS DREYFUS, ASHBY & CO NEW YORK N.Y. 10165

750 M... (25,4 FL. OZ.) ALCOHOL 12% BY VOLUME, CONTAINS SULFIT...

2002

NEUCHA...

APPELLATION D'ORIG...

CAV...

CHÂTEAU

AUVER...

THIERRY GROS...

PETIT-FILS D'ALOYS

PROPRIÉTAIRE

2012 AUVERNI...

750ml e   ENCAVAGE FONDÉ EN 1603

RECIPES

FONDUE WITH TRUFFLES

Cheese fondue isn't a light dish; the Swiss maintain that a coup de milieu—that is, a glass of kirsch drunk halfway through the meal—aids digestion, as well as one's general outlook on life.

Serves 4

1	clove garlic, peeled and halved
¼	cup dry white wine
2	tbsp. heavy cream
6	ounces gruyère, grated
6	ounces emmentaler, grated
2	tsp. cornstarch

Pinch nutmeg

Salt and freshly ground white pepper

½	ounce white truffle, cleaned
1	baguette, cut into cubes

1. Rub the inside of a fondue pot or medium saucepan with the garlic. Discard any unused garlic. Add the wine and cream and bring to a boil over medium heat.

2. Add the cheese to the pot, one handful at a time, and cook, stirring constantly until cheese is melted. Sift in the cornstarch and stir until incorporated. Add the nutmeg and season to taste with salt and pepper. Shave the truffles over the fondue. Keep fondue warm over lowest heat. Serve with bread cubes.

SWISS RÖSTI WITH CRÈME FRAÎCHE AND CAVIAR

One of the traditional foods of Switzerland, rösti is essentially a potato pancake—delicious on its own, but much better with a little caviar and crème fraîche.

Serves 4 to 8

1	pound waxy potatoes, peeled

Salt and freshly ground black pepper

2	tbsp. butter
6	tbsp. vegetable oil
8	tsp. crème fraîche
1	ounce caviar

1. Grate the potatoes on the large holes of a box grater. Put half the potatoes in the center of a clean tea towel and squeeze out as much water as possible. Transfer potatoes to a bowl and repeat the process with the remaining potatoes. Season potatoes with salt and pepper and set aside.

2. Heat 1 tbsp. butter and 3 tbsp. oil in a medium non-stick skillet over medium heat. Divide the potato mixture into 16 equal portions (each should be about 1½ inches in diameter when flattened). Arrange half of the portions in the skillet about 1 inch apart and gently press down on each mound with a spatula to flatten. Cook, undisturbed, until golden and crisp, about 5 minutes. Carefully turn potatoes and continue cooking on second side until golden and cooked through, about 5 minutes more. Repeat process with remaining butter, oil and potatoes. Keep rösti warm in a 200° F oven.

3. When ready to serve, garnish each rösti with a ½ tsp. crème fraîche and some of the caviar.

BROILED LOBSTER

Lobsters aren't exactly Swiss—in fact, they're not Swiss at all, Switzerland being entirely landlocked. But you can certainly find them in St. Moritz.

Serves 2 to 4

Salt
Two 1½-pound live lobsters
4   tbsp. heavy cream
Freshly ground black pepper

1. Preheat the broiler. Bring a large pot of salted water to a boil over high heat. Add the lobsters and boil until just cooked through, 4 minutes. Drain the lobsters and shock in a bowl of ice water to prevent them from cooking any more. Once the lobsters are cool, remove the claws and set aside. Using a large kitchen knife, cut the lobsters in half lengthwise and transfer to a baking sheet, cut side up. Crack the claws and transfer to the baking sheet.

2. Pour 1 tbsp. of cream over each lobster half and season to taste with salt and pepper. Broil the lobsters until cooked through and lightly browned, 6 to 8 minutes.

PINEAPPLE TART

Pineapples don't get any sweeter once they're picked, so make sure you purchase a ripe one. It should feel heavy and be golden in color, with deep green flexible leaves. Also, turn it over and smell the base—it should have a ripe, sweet scent.

Serves 8

1   large pineapple, trimmed, peeled, quartered
         and cored
4   tbsp. butter
⅓   cup sugar
½   pound frozen puff pastry, thawed
Flour

1. Preheat oven to 350° F. Cut the pineapple crosswise into 1-inch pieces. Melt the butter in a heavy 10-inch skillet over medium-high heat. Add the pineapple and cook, turning occasionally, until lightly golden, 10 to 15 minutes. Sprinkle on the sugar and continue cooking until the sugar turns mahogany brown and pineapple is soft, another 10 to 15 minutes.

2. Roll the pastry out on a lightly floured surface to a 12-inch circle. Drape the pastry over the pineapple and fold in the excess to create a crust. Bake until pastry is golden brown, about 30 minutes. Remove the tart from the oven and set aside for 5 minutes, then set a plate over the pastry and carefully invert tart onto the plate. Serve warm or at room temperature.

RICH CHOCOLATE MOUSSE

A good Swiss bittersweet chocolate (the Lindt brand is widely available in the United States) would be ideal for this rich chocolate confection.

Serves 6

6	ounces bittersweet chocolate, finely chopped
1	cup heavy cream
1	tbsp. brandy
3	eggs, at room temperature
5	tbsp. sugar

1. Put 2 cups water into a medium saucepan and bring to a simmer over medium heat. Stir the chocolate and ½ cup of the heavy cream together in a large heatproof bowl. Set the bowl over the simmering water and stir frequently until the chocolate is melted. Stir in the brandy and remove the bowl from the heat.

2. Whisk the eggs, 3 tbsp. sugar and 2 tbsp. water together in another large heatproof bowl and set over the saucepan of simmering water. Reduce the heat to medium-low and cook, stirring constantly, until the temperature reaches 160° F on an instant-read thermometer. Remove the bowl from the heat and beat with an electric mixer on high speed until the mixture becomes the consistency of whipped cream, about 5 minutes. Fold one cup of the melted chocolate mixture into the egg mixture then pour the egg mixture into the chocolate mixture, folding until well mixed.

3. Divide the chocolate mousse between six 4-ounce dessert cups. Cover cups with plastic wrap and refrigerate until chilled. Once ready to serve, whip the remaining cream and remaining sugar together until stiff peaks form. Garnish each mousse with some of the whipped cream.

STRAWBERRY MILLEFEUILLE

Millefeuille *means "thousand layers" in French, referring to the flaky pastry that surrounds the creamy filling in this elegant dessert.*

Serves 8

1	vanilla bean, split lengthwise
3	cups milk
8	egg yolks
1	cup granulated sugar
½	cup flour
¼	cup cornstarch
1	pound frozen puff pastry, thawed
3	tbsp. confectioners' sugar
1	pint fresh strawberries, hulled and halved

1. Scrape the seeds from the vanilla and add the seeds and pod to a heavy saucepan. Add the milk and bring to a boil over medium heat. Whisk the egg yolks and granulated sugar together until pale yellow and thick. Sift the flour and cornstarch into the egg mixture and whisk until smooth. Remove and discard the vanilla pod from the milk. Add 1 cup of the hot milk to the egg yolk mixture, whisking constantly, then return entire mixture to the pan. Reduce heat to medium-low and cook, whisking constantly, until mixture becomes the consistency of thick pudding, 6 to 8 minutes. Transfer the pastry cream to a large bowl, cover the surface with plastic wrap to prevent a skin from forming and refrigerate until chilled.

2. Preheat oven to 450° F. Line two baking sheets with parchment paper. Divide the pastry in half. Roll each half out on a lightly floured surface to a 9-by-13-inch rectangle. Transfer each rectangle to the prepared baking sheets and prick all over with the tines of a fork. Cover each pastry with another sheet of parchment paper and then cover parchment with another baking sheet. Bake until golden around the edges, 10 to 12 minutes. Remove the top baking sheets and top sheets of parchment and continue baking, uncovered, until golden brown, 2 to 3 minutes. Transfer to a cooling rack.

3. Trim each pastry down to an 8-by-12-inch rectangle, saving trimmings. Cut each rectangle in half lengthwise, making four 4-by-12-inch rectangles. Put the pastry cream into a pastry bag. Arrange one rectangle onto a serving platter, then pipe some of the pastry cream over the entire surface of the pastry. Cover the pastry cream with another pastry rectangle and repeat the process two more times, ending with pastry. Crush pastry trimmings and press into the sides of the cake. Dust the top of the cake with confectioners' sugar and garnish with strawberries. Refrigerate for 30 minutes to allow cake to set before serving.

RECIPE INDEX